ISBN 978-1-332-14161-6
PIBN 10290273

Similar Books Are Available from
www.forgottenbooks.com

Gentlemen:

Enclosed please find $

for which send me the articles liste

List Number	Quantity	Description of Article
		DEC -4 1916

SPALDING ATHLETIC LIBRARY

SPALDING OFFICIAL ANNUALS

No. 1. SPALDING'S OFFICIAL BASE BALL GUIDE. . . . . Price 10c.

No. 2. SPALDING'S OFFICIAL FOOT BALL GUIDE. . . . . Price 10c.

No. 6. SPALDING'S OFFICIAL ICE HOCKEY GUIDE. . . . . Price 10c.

No. 7. SPALDING'S OFFICIAL BASKET BALL GUIDE. . . . Price 10c.

No. 7A. SPALDING'S OFFICIAL WOMEN'S BASKET BALL GUIDE. Price 10c.

No. 9. SPALDING'S OFFICIAL INDOOR BASE BALL GUIDE. . Price 10c.

No. 12A. SPALDING'S OFFICIAL ATHLETIC RULES. . . . . Price 10c.

No. 1R. SPALDING'S OFFICIAL ATHLETIC ALMANAC. . . Price 25c.

No. 3R. SPALDING'S OFFICIAL GOLF GUIDE. . . . . . . Price 25c.

No. 55R. SPALDING'S OFFICIAL SOCCER FOOT BALL GUIDE. . Price 25c.

No. 57R. SPALDING'S LAWN TENNIS ANNUAL. . . . . . . Price 25c.

No. 59R. SPALDING'S OFFICIAL BASE BALL RECORD. . . . Price 25c.

Specially Bound Series of Athletic Handbooks

Flexible binding. Mailed postpaid on receipt of 50 cents each number.

No. 501L. STROKES AND SCIENCE OF LAWN TENNIS
No. 502L. HOW TO PLAY GOLF
No. 503L. HOW TO PLAY FOOT BALL
No. 504L. ART OF SKATING
No. 505L. GET WELL—KEEP WELL
No. 506L. HOW TO LIVE 100 YEARS
No. 507L. HOW TO WRESTLE
No. 508L. HOW TO PLAY LAWN TENNIS; HOW TO PLAY TENNIS FOR BEGINNERS
No. 509L. BOXING
No. 510L. DUMB BELL EXERCISES
No. 511L. JIU JITSU
No. 512L. SPEED SWIMMING
No. 513L. WINTER SPORTS
No. 514L. HOW TO BOWL
No. 515L. HOW TO SWIM AND COMPETITIVE DIVING.
No. 516L. SCHOOL TACTICS AND MAZE RUNNING; CHILDREN'S GAMES.
No. 517L. TEN AND TWENTY MINUTE EXERCISES
No. 518L. INDOOR AND OUTDOOR GYMNASTIC GAMES
No. 519L. SPALDING'S OFFICIAL BASE BALL GUIDE
No. 520L. SPALDING'S OFFICIAL FOOT BALL GUIDE
No. 521L. SPALDING'S OFFICIAL BASKET BALL GUIDE
No. 522L. GOLF FOR GIRLS
No. 523L. HOW TO PLAY BASE BALL; HOW TO UMPIRE; HOW TO MANAGE A TEAM, ETC.
No. 524L. SPALDING'S LAWN TENNIS ANNUAL
No. 525L. HOW TO PITCH; READY RECKONER OF BASE BALL PERCENTAGES
No. 526L. HOW TO CATCH; HOW TO BAT

In addition to above, any 25 cent "Red Cover" book listed in Spalding's Athletic Library will be bound in flexible binding for 50 cents each; or any two 10 cent "Green Cover" or "Blue Cover" books in one volume for 50 cents.

(Continued on the next page.)

SPALDING ATHLETIC LIBRARY

Group I.   Base Ball

"Blue Cover" Series, each number 10c.

No. 1   Spalding's Official Base Ball Guide
No. 202 How to Play Base Ball
No. 219 Ready Reckoner of Base Ball
No. 223 How to Bat   [Percentages
No. 224 How to Play the Outfield
No. 225 How to Play First Base
No. 226 How to Play Second Base
No. 227 How to Play Third Base
No. 228 How to Play Shortstop
No. 229 How to Catch
No. 230 How to Pitch
No. 231
- How to Organize a Base Ball League   [Club
- How to Organize a Base Ball Club
- How to Manage a Base Ball Club
- How to Train a Base Ball Team
- How to Captain a Base Ball
- How to Umpire   [Team
- Technical Base Ball Terms

No. 232 How to Run Bases
No. 350 How to Score
No. 355 Minor League Base Ball Guide
No. 356 Official Book National League of Prof. Base Ball Clubs
No. 9   Spalding's Official Indoor Base Ball Guide

"Red Cover" Series, each number 25c.

No. 59R. Official Base Ball Record (including College records)

Group II.   Foot Ball

"Blue Cover" Series, each number 10c.

No. 2   Spalding's Official Foot Ball
No. 335 How to Play Rugby   [Guide
No. 358 Official College Soccer Guide

"Red Cover" Series, each number 25c.

No. 39R. How to Play Soccer
No. 47R. How to Play Foot Ball
No. 55R. Spalding's Official Soccer Foot Ball Guide

Group III.   Tennis

"Blue Cover" Series, each number 10c.

No. 157 How to Play Lawn Tennis
No. 363 Tennis Errors and the Remedies.

"Green Cover" Series, each number 10c.

No. 1P. How to Play Tennis—For Beginners. By P. A. Vaile.

"Red Cover" Series, each number 25c.

No. 2R. Strokes and Science of Lawn Tennis   [tralasia
No. 42R. Davis Cup Contests in Aus-
No. 57R. Spalding's Lawn Tennis Annual

Group IV.   Golf

"Green Cover" Series, each number 10c.

No. 2P. How to Learn Golf

"Red Cover" Series, each number 25c.

No. 3R. Spalding's Official Golf
No. 4R. How to Play Golf   [Guide
No. 63R. Golf for Girls

Group V.   Basket Ball

"Blue Cover" Series, each number 10c.

No. 7   Spalding's Official Basket Ball Guide
No. 7A Spalding's Official Women's Basket Ball Guide
No. 193 How to Play Basket Ball

Group VI. Skating and Winter Sports

"Blue Cover" Series, each number 10c.

No. 6   Spalding's Official Ice Hockey
No. 14 Curling   [Guide

"Red Cover" Series, each number 25c.

No. 8R. The Art of Skating
No. 20R. How to Play Ice Hockey
No. 28R. Winter Sports
No. 72R. Figure Skating for Women

Group VII.   Field and Track Athletics

"Blue Cover" Series, each number 10c.

No. 12A Spalding's Official Athletic Rules
No. 27 College Athletics
No. 55 Official Sporting Rules
No. 87 Athletic Primer
No. 156 Athletes' Guide
No. 178 How to Train for Bicycling
No. 182 All Around Athletics
No. 255 How to Run 100 Yards
No. 302 Y. M. C. A. Official Handbook
No. 311 Marathon Running
No. 342 Walking for Health and Competition
No. 362 Track, Relay and Cross Country Rules of the National Collegiate Athletic Ass'n.

"Green Cover" Series, each number 10c.

No. 3P. How to Become an Athlete By James E. Sullivan
No. 4P. How to Sprint

"Red Cover" Series, each number 25c.

No. 1R. Spalding's Official Athletic Almanac
No. 17R. Olympic Games, Stockholm, 1912   [book
No. 45R. Intercollegiate Official Hand-
No. 48R. Distance and Cross Country Running
No. 70R. How to Become a Weight Thrower

(Continued on the next page.)

SPALDING ATHLETIC LIBRARY

Group VIII. School Athletics
"*Blue Cover*" *Series, each number 10c.*
No. 246 Athletic Training for School-
No. 331 Schoolyard Athletics [boys
"*Red Cover*" *Series, each number 25c.*
No. 61R. School Tactics and Maze Run-
ning; Children's Games
No. 66R. Calisthenic Drills and Fancy
Marching and P h y s i c a l
Training for the School
and Class Room
No. 71R. Public Schools A t h l e t i c
League Official Handbook

Group IX. Water Sports
"*Blue Cover*" *Series, each number 10c.*
No. 128 How to Row
No. 129 Water Polo   [Guide
No. 361 Intercollegiate S w i m m i n g
"*Red Cover*" *Series, each number 25c.*
No. 36R. Speed Swimming
No. 37R. How to Swim and Competi-
tive Diving
No. 60R. Canoeing and Camping

Group X. Athletic Games for Women and Girls
"*Blue Cover*" *Series, each number 10c.*
No. 7A Spalding's Official Women's
Basket Ball Guide
No. 314 Girls' Athletics
"*Red Cover*" *Series, each number 25c.*
No. 38R. Field Hockey
No. 41R. Newcomb
No. 63R. Golf for Girls
No. 69R. Athletics for Girls

Group XI. Lawn and Field Games
"*Blue Cover*" *Series, each number 10c.*
No. 167 Quoits
No. 170 Push Ball
No. 180 Ring Hockey
No. 199 Equestrian Polo
No. 201 How to Play Lacrosse
No. 207 Lawn Bowls
"*Red Cover*" *Series, each number, 25c.*
No. 6R. Cricket, and How to Play It

Group XII. Miscellaneous Games
"*Blue Cover*" *Series, each number 10c.*
No. 13 American Game of Hand Ball
No. 364 Volley Ball
"*Red Cover*" *Series, each number 25c.*
No. 43R. Archery, R o q u e, Croquet,
English Croquet, Lawn H o c k e y,
Tether Ball, Clock Golf, Golf-Croquet,
Hand Tennis, Hand Polo, W i c k e t
Polo, Badminton, Drawing R o o m
H o c k e y, Garden Hockey, Basket
Goal, Volley Ball Rules and Pin Ball
No. 49R. How to Bowl
No. 50R. Court Games

Group XIII. Manly Sports
"*Blue Cover*" *Series, each number 10c.*
No. 191 How to Punch the Bag
No. 282 Roller Skating Guide
"*Red Cover*" *Series, each number 25c.*
No. 11R. Fencing Foil Work Illustrat-
No. 19R. Professional Wrestling [ed
No. 21R. Jiu Jitsu
No. 25R. Boxing
No. 30R. The Art of Fencing
No. 65R. How to Wrestle

Group XIV. Calisthenics
"*Blue Cover*" *Series, each number 10c.*
No. 214 Graded C a l i s t h e n i c s and
Dumb Bell Drills
"*Red Cover*" *Series, each number 25c.*
No. 10R. Single Stick Drill
No. 16R. Team Wand Drill
No. 22R. Indian Clubs a n d Dumb
Bells and Pulley Weights
No. 24R. Dumb Bell Exercises

Group XV. Gymnastics
"*Blue Cover*" *Series, each number 10c.*
No. 124 How to Become a Gymnast
No. 254 Barnjum Bar Bell Drill
No. 287 Fancy Dumb Bell and March-
ing Drills
"*Red Cover*" *Series, each number 25c.*
No. 14R. Trapeze, Long Horse and
Rope Exercises
No. 34R. Grading of Gym. Exercises
No. 40R. Indoor and Outdoor Gym-
nastic Games
No. 52R. Pyramid Building w i t h
Wands, Chairs and Ladders
No. 56R. Tumbling for Amateurs and
Ground Tumbling
No. 67R. Exercises on the Side Horse:
Exercises on the Flying
Rings.
No. 68R. Horizontal Bar Exercises;
Exercises on Parallel Bars

Group XVI. Home Exercising
"*Blue Cover*" *Series, each number 10c.*
No. 161 Ten Minutes' Exercise for
No. 185 Hints on Health [Busy Men
No. 325 Twenty-Minute Exercises
"*Red Cover*" *Series, each number 25c.*
No. 7R. Physical Training Simplified
No. 9R. How to Live 100 Years
No. 23R. Get Well: Keep Well
No. 33R. Tensing Exercises
No. 51R. 285 Health Answers
No. 54R. Medicine Ball E x e r c i s e s,
Indigestion Treated by Gymnastics,
Physical Education and Hygiene
No. 62R. The Care of the Body
No. 64R. Muscle Building; Health by
Muscular Gymnastics

ANY OF THE ABOVE BOOKS MAILED POSTPAID UPON RECEIPT OF PRICE

FIG. 1—CORRECT STARTING POSITION.

SPALDING'S ATHLETIC LIBRARY
Group XIV   No. 191

HOW TO PUNCH THE BAG

BY

YOUNG CORBETT

With an Article on

FANCY BAG PUNCHING

NEW YORK
AMERICAN SPORTS PUBLISHING COMPANY
21 WARREN STREET

FIG. 2—STRAIGHT LEFT HAND—THE CORRECT WAY.

BAG PUNCHING AS A BENEFICIAL AND ATTRACTIVE EXERCISE

Many forms of exercise are indulged in by folk desirous of improving their physical condition, but none of them is more attractive and at the same time more beneficial than bag punching. Here is a recreation, simple and inexpensive, awarding splendid means for the development of bodily powers, and indulgence in which, rewards with symmetry, grace and strength obtainable in no other way.

Did you ever punch the bag? If so, you are well aware of the truth of the foregoing statements; if you never have tried this unsurpassed exercise, you have before you a pleasure as valuable as it is fascinating, and that is saying a great deal. One of the beauties of bag punching is that it may be indulged in by men, women and children alike; another is that the apparatus is thoroughly adapted to use in any home, no matter how small—even if the prospective enthusiast lives in a hall bedroom in a city apartment, or in an attic room in some antiquated farm house.

As for the actual benefits to be derived from punching the bag—well, a book could be written on this subject alone. From the view point of the man who is lacking physically the exercise is nothing short of fondest imaginings of the idealist.

Arms, shoulders, hands, wrists, the neck, and legs are brought into play individually and in combination in bag punching. Aside from the development in these parts of the body, the shoulders are made square and upright, the chest is broadened, the eye quickened, and the brain stimulated. The circulation of the blood in all parts of the body is vastly improved. The direct result is a new being for the bag puncher. He goes into nature's storehouse and by tendering exercise in payment, receives a supply of health and vigor, just as he would enter a shop and purchase a new suit of clothes in return for "coin of the realm,"

FIG. 3—STRAIGHT LEFT HAND—THE WRONG WAY.

Does the end justify the means? Where is the person who would answer in the negative? He is as difficult to find as was of old the much sought for Philosopher's Stone, which, according to tradition, would transform into purest gold whatsoever it touched.

Accomplished athletes, too, find value in the punching bag. Hundreds of them consider it indispensable in maintaining the muscles developed in other branches of sport. Inactivity, of course, is the bane of the athlete's existence. A month or two of idleness lamentably deteriorates the finest set of muscles that ever adorned a human frame, and boxers, gymnasts, foot ball and base ball players, etc., etc., have found the punching bag to be one of the best agencies obtainable for keeping themselves in condition, and in promoting agility and endurance. Then, too, the element of self-defence creeps in, and in fact plays a prominent part in the usefulness of the apparatus under consideration. The bag puncher finds that he can use his hands to advantage in emergencies. He is a dangerous man with whom to trifle. His self-reliance and confidence make him all the more strongly fortified. Boxers find the inflated spheroid invaluable in training and most of them are experts in the manipulation of it.

The bag is a prominent object in the training quarters of every knight of the padded mitts. There never was a boxer or a fighter yet who has not used it, and used it but to praise.

The use of punching bags has increased tremendously during the last few years. This fact in itself is significant, for the people of this day and generation are not prone to throw away time and money on worthless things. Popularity denotes merit invariably in these matter-of-fact twentieth-century times, whether persons, places or pastimes are concerned. In every well-equipped gymnasium is found at least one bag punching apparatus, and seldom indeed is the rapid rap-rap-rap of the bounding leather ball missing among the sounds familiar to the frequenters of buildings devoted to all-around recreation.

Physical directors in athletic clubs, Young Men's Christian

FIG. 4—STRAIGHT RIGHT HAND PUNCH.

Association "gyms," etc., state unhesitatingly that the punching bag oftentimes brings them new members and that the interest of the devotees of this sport rarely wanes. In fact, "once a bag puncher always a bag puncher" may well be said to be the case. Just what element of this form of exercise is responsible for its fascinations is difficult to determine. Whether it is the permissible unlimited pummeling of an imaginary antagonist; the realization of the benefits accruing from its use, or the rythm in the lively rebounding of the inflated bag, cannot be stated with any degree of certainty, but at any rate, the fascination is there, and he that seeks will find it. It lures the mere casual puncher on and on until he is as deeply engrossed in the sport as a school boy is in playing his first game of marbles.

The writer has a friend, a New Yorker, who recently chose to had passed before his two younger brothers, aged seventeen and nineteen, began to endeavor to solve its mysteries. They were not slow in learning. Soon they monopolized the bag almost entirely. They rose early in the morning to take turns at punching it. They would hurry through their dinner in the evening to go at it again. My friend endured this state of affairs for about two weeks with nothing more than an occasional protest, but finally, however, was added the straw that broke the camel's back.

One afternoon he left his business early and hastened home to have a half hour's practice without interruption. He knew his brothers would not be on hand at this particular time. Entering the house, a familiar rapping, tapping sound smote his ears and there before him was his sister, about twenty years of age, pounding away like a veteran. My friend dropped into a chair, exclaiming, "Well, *this* is the limit."

"But, Harry," was the fair culprit's response, "I've been doing this for days and days. It's the finest sport I've ever had, and what is more, I'm as good a bag puncher as you are." This last remark proved to be true, and poor, persecuted Harry was eventually forced to buy a bag for his sister, who, **by the way,**

FIG. 5—IMPROPER POSITION OF THE HEAD. ALWAYS WATCH THE BAG WHEN YOU STRIKE. DO NOT LOOK AWAY.

afterward inducted several of her girl friends into the secrets of the art. .

And so the punching bag wields its magic power. Young and old, the fair and the unfair are drawn into the net, but happily only to be benefited thereby.

Noticeable features in the makeup of the bag puncher are the grace of his carriage and the uniformity of his development. No muscle seems to be abnormal and consequently unsightly. He is easily singled out in a crowd by his ease of movement. These attributes go to form personal attractiveness and magnetism, without which any man is handicapped, no matter what may be his occupation or station in life. The man with an air of energy and accomplishment is the one who impresses and compels. Should he lack these qualities a month or two of systematic bag punching will supply them.

The value of the strength and other physical assets given by bag punching cannot be overestimated. A man's greatest possession is his body, therefore he should seek to make it as close to perfect as possible. The weakling has no chance to win in the strenuous commercial, professional, social and political campaigns of to-day and the sooner this fact is realized the better.

FIG. 6—MOST DANGEROUS WAY TO PUNCH A BAG. NEVER STRIKE
TOWARD A WALL.

GENERAL HINTS TO PUNCHERS OF THE BAG, AND SPECIAL REFERENCE TO BEGINNERS

Some experts attempt to say just how much a punching bag should be elevated or lowered. Each man, however, is the best judge for himself in reference to this matter. The spheroid should be allowed to swing freely and at the same time not so much as to cause it to rebound wildly. Your height and reach are to be considered in lowering or raising it. Do not punch the bag for a lengthy period without resting, at least until you are well advanced. At first, ten minutes' punching, with from three to five minutes' rest, will be found advisable. Later you can increase the length of your exercising periods until finally you will become almost indefatigable, unless you accelerate speed unduly.

First learn to perform the different blows slowly and accurately. Form a style, just as you should do in boxing, running or jumping, and stick to it so long as it is correct and adapted to your physical characteristics. Should you start in, while yet a beginner, to hit the bag rapidly—and most tyros are likely to commit this fault—you will surely lose accuracy and work into an improper style, which, as time goes on, and you still persist in it, will prevent you from ever becoming expert, or even passably proficient. An ounce of prevention is worth at least a ton of cure in this instance, so let speed alone until you are sure of yourself.

Always clench your fist properly. Press the points of the fingers into the palms and keep the knuckles on a straight line. Unless you observe this rule closely a finger or two will invariably project beyond the others, making likely dislocation or other painful and incapacitating injury. In addition an improperly closed fist will send the bag out of its intended course, thus breaking up your exercise, making necessary a new start. Clench your fist as does a prize fighter when he dons the gloves.

Fig. 7—A VALUELESS BLOW.

You may or may not use bag punching gloves, as you choose. You had best procure a pair or two of them however, while learning the art. They will assist you materially in delivering even blows, but they will make your work somewhat slower than bare-handed tactics. After you have progressed, to some extent, try punching without gloves. Your knuckles will suffer at first but finally the skin will become toughened so that you will not be inconvenienced.

Your costume, if you punch the bag in a gymnasium, should be light, cool and unencumbersome. A sleeveless jersey and knee or full length tights, with either high or low shoes, will suffice. If you desire to reduce weight wear a sweater while at work. At home almost any kind of a costume will suffice. After exercising—if in a gymnasium—put on a sweater, or if you have enough work for the time being, take a shower bath. Begin with warm water, or hot if you desire, and finish with the coldest to be had, especially in winter weather take care to end a bath with cold water. It will close the pores of the skin and prevent you from being chilled when going into the brisk air. A spirited rub down with a rough towel, or if you so desire, an alcohol or a witch hazel rub, will make you feel as though you had quaffed of the water of the famous spring of eternal youth for which Ponce de Leon is said to have searched unavailingly in Florida a couple of centuries or so ago.

Beginners should always be content to advance slowly, at least until the actual rudiments are mastered. Of course all ambitious youths desire to obtain the maximum of proficiency in the minimum of time. This is all very well, a very commendable trait to be sure, but remember that the lesson of moderation, while difficult to learn, pays in the end. You cannot learn to punch the bag in a week even though you neither eat nor sleep. Give me two pupils, one careful, painstaking at the start, and the other self-willed and over-anxious, who practices a dozen different blows in as many minutes, and I'll wager every cent I own that the first named will know more about the practice of bag punching in a month than the independent, variable, inconstant young man could show you in six months.

Another hint for beginners is that you should not set your heart on learning fancy blows too early in the game. They are splendid pastimes when the fundamental principles are thoroughly mastered and assimilated. They require advanced dexterity and understanding, also unceasing practice and study. When poorly executed—as is sure to be the case with novices—they fall so flat that spectators will consider you an amateur of the greenest sort.

Learn to breathe regularly while punching the bag. Inhale and exhale at timed intervals, filling the lungs almost to their capacity on the intake, and expel the air without straining yourself. You can increase your chest measurements noticeably in a short time. By forcing too·much into your lungs suddenly, however, or exhaling too violently, you will become dizzy. So, therefore, develop your breathing capacity gradually.

Do not exercise with heavy weights or other ponderous apparatus if you intend to become an expert bag puncher. The muscular fibre thus formed gives you coarse, binding tissues that will rob you of suppleness. Light dumbbells, light Indian clubs, from one to three pounds; chest weights, rowing machines, etc., etc., are admirably suited to the bag puncher's needs. Hand ball, boxing, basket ball, etc., are excellent accompaniments to your athletic curriculum.

Keep your finger nails trimmed moderately short, especially if you punch the bag without gloves. Sometimes the bag accidentally strikes a nail and breaks it, causing a bothersome, painful, slow-healing wound, and at the same time making the fingers unsightly. Do not punch the bag directly after a heavy meal. You will speedily induce indigestion by so doing. Unless you have eaten sparingly wait at least an hour and half after dining before beginning your work.

Should you punch the bag at home and desire to go to bed on finishing, do not take a cold bath. Cold water will stimulate your system to such an extent that you will be unable to go to sleep readily. Instead, bathe in warm water, and do not rub yourself vigorously as such action will also prove stimulating.

Merely dry yourself so that you will not be absolutely damp, and then go immediately to bed. You will drop off to sleep without difficulty. An old German physician once told me that by prescribing this simple remedy he had cured scores of cases of insomnia.

FIG. 8—A GOOD ONE-ARM EXERCISE, IN WHICH EITHER ELBOW
MAY BE USED.

HOW TO PUNCH THE BAG

THE PROPER POSITION.

(Fig. 1.)

When ready to punch the bag take a position that gives you ample place to strike it without straining or over-reaching. At the same time do not make the mistake of standing so close to it as to crowd yourself. Freedom and ease of movement are essential points to consider. Assume a fighting pose. Straighten your back, thrust your shoulders to the rear gracefully, raise your left hand to about the height of your chin, bring up the right to guard, clench your fist with the knuckles even, as previously instructed, and advance the left foot before the right. The position of the hands and feet should be altered to suit varying blows. Under ordinary circumstances hold in the point of the chin, just as in boxing. The differences in the posture for the various blows will be explained in the detailed descriptions which are to follow.

THE LEFT LEAD.

(Fig. 2.)

The novice should begin his punching bag operations by learning the two fundamental, and at the same time two simplest blows. They are the left lead and the right lead. As in boxing, both these leads are very important. We will consider the left lead first.

Stand from two and a half to three and a half feet from the bag, which should swing on a level with the nose. Stepping forward as you would to deliver the same blow in boxing, lead directly with your left from the shoulder, hitting the centre of the bag. The head should be inclined slightly to the right to avoid a counter. Bring your right hand and forearm up across, and close to your chest, as defence against an imaginary return

FIG. 9—LEFT HAND HOOK.

blow, and put as much weight into the stroke as possible with out throwing yourself off your balance. Gauge distance accurately. Quick as a flash spring back into your original position, with the left foot advanced as in boxing, and repeat the blow. Learn to hit with lightning rapidity, and to regain your position without the loss of a moment. Should you hit the bag a glancing blow it will come back at an angle to its rightful course and possibly hit the striker smartly in the face. If you have not hit it squarely, duck. The practice of ducking will also help you in learning to box.

Of course if you hit the bag violently you will be unable to again strike it on the first rebound. Let it bounce, say, three times before repeating a blow. Thus you will have opportunity to develop accuracy and good form. By persevering in the practice of the left lead, as is likewise true of all the other strokes, you can develop the blow into a very powerful form of attack.

Many boxers are weak with their left. Ineffective jabs are the best results they produce with it. This shortcoming would speedily be remedied by the generous use of the punching bag.

Hit the bag with the face of the knuckles and do not let the fist go wide like a swing—swings will be considered later.

Make the blow clean cut, perfect in itself, putting the full force of the shoulder and back into it. Keep your eye on the ball, watching its every move and variation. Moreover, be sure that it is inflated to the limit. The punching of a flabby bag is about as much value as boxing would be with stuffed pillow cases taking the place of gloves.

THE STRAIGHT LEFT LEAD—INCORRECT WAY.
(Fig. 3.)

Many years of punching bags fall into an incorrect method of holding the fist as it strikes the bag. In illustration No. 3 this fault is shown. By observing closely you will see that my left fist is turned so that the thumb is to the right, the palm

FIG. 10—ALTERNATING SHORT RIGHT AND LEFT HOOKS.

of the hand downward. Instead the thumb ought to turn upward, which action will place the knuckles toward the left, the clenched palm to the right.

Blows delivered in a faulty manner of this sort lack force, and in addition in a ring contest would be very apt to expose your wrist to breaking. Hold your fist in this improper way and draw it well back as though you intended to land a heavy blow. You will immediately perceive that the position is awkard and that your shoulder is subjected to an unnecessary strain. Authoritative judges of pugilism, and boxers I have met in matches, say that I am a very hard hitter. The results of my battles would seem to indicate their opinion to be true, and I say unreservedly that whatever ability I may have as a powerful and effective hitter is due to my learning to deliver blows in the best possible way, according to the requirements of good form. Accuracy is never a drawback to a boxer or a bag puncher. The turning of the palm downward also deprives the forearm of considerable of leverage and the practice will tell heavily against any man. On reading these words you may say, "This is all very well, but I cause the bag to rebound straighter by turning the palm to the floor." If you have learned this, the wrong way to punch, change your tactics instantly, no matter how agreeable they are to you. They will be satisfactory only temporarily at the best. Remember the words of the immortal Davy Crockett, when he said, "Be sure you're right, then go ahead."

The foregoing criticism applies also to all other blows in the bag puncher's category. I merely chose the left lead as one instance among a great many.

THE STRAIGHT RIGHT HAND PUNCH.
(Fig. 4.)

In the straight right hand lead, step out with the right foot, placing it about eighteen inches to the right, and about fourteen inches in front of the left foot. Hold the left hand in front of, and close to either the abdomen, chest or chin as a guard, and

FIG. 11—HALF UPPER-CUT WITH RIGHT HAND.

shoot the right out snappily from the shoulder, hitting the bag squarely, as in the left lead. You can maintain this position and hit the bag repeatedly on say every third rebound, or else you may step back into your original waiting position after every blow. By the latter method you will obtain much valuable training in footwork.

Footwork is one of the principal dependencies of the boxer, and anything that helps him develop his ability in this line is valuable. The straight right is one of the most powerful and effective blows that can be delivered by the human hand. Two handed fighters use it with telling results. The fact that its delivery leaves a man comparatively open to attack, however, makes it unpopular with some fighters.

Throw your weight into this blow, just as you should in others. I would also suggest that you incline or duck your head to the left, not pronouncedly, however, to avoid what in boxing would be a counter. When you have mastered the details of the right lead, alternate it with the left lead, executing first one stroke and then the other. If the alternate movement seems awkward in the beginning, do not become discouraged, but persevere, and after a few trials it will prove very easy, and assuredly more interesting than either of the individual blows in themselves.

AN IMPROPER POSITION OF THE HEAD, AND WHICH PREVENTS THE PUNCHER FROM WATCHING THE BAG.

(Fig. 5.)

In bag punching, as in all other pastimes conducted on a scientific basis, there are many things to avoid. One of the several points of this nature that I will mention in this book is the position of the head while in action. Do not turn your head completely away from the bag at any time for you will then be unable to watch it closely. Watch the bag continually, even as you would an opponent in the ring. Of course there are various occasions when you should duck, or otherwise avoid the

FIG. 12—HALF UPPERCUT WITH LEFT HAND.

bounding ball, but unless you are striking the bag with the back of the head, KEEP YOUR EYES ON IT. Think what a beautifully small chance you would have in a boxing match if you turned your head away from your antagonst. He would land on you so quickly that you would not be likely to come back to earth for several minutes at the very least. Remember that every careless habit you form while punching the bag will surely follow you and handicap you when you don the mitts.

A DANGEROUS PRACTICE—HITTING TOWARD A WALL.
(Fig. 6.)

Do not strike toward a wall when puching a bag. Should you do so and happen to miss the inflated object, your hand will strike the hard substance with a disastrous effect. I do not mean that you will damage some landlord's plaster or wooden partition—no, not for a moment. You will on the contrary lame your fist and indeed will be in great luck if you escape without fracturing a bone or two. The hands of the boxer and the bag puncher alike are his stock in trade. You have possibly observed that fighters, wrestlers, etc., take pronounced care of hands and fingers. To disable them will often mean bankruptcy and perhaps loss of prestige.

A VALUELESS BLOW THAT SOME BAG PUNCHERS ARE FOND OF USING.
(Fig. 7.)

Oftentimes you will see a chap go to a punching bag, double his fists and press them close together, palms inward. He will then proceed to use them as a battering ram to pound the bag violently. The bag rebounds, striking his two fists, of course, at the same time. What good is there to be derived from this maneuver? I will offer a prize of a package of Joss sticks to the first one sending me an answer that can be given serious consideration. There is not enough tax on any particular muscles to develop them. Neither does the "stunt" promote agility or quickness

FIG. 13—FULL SWING WITH THE RIGHT.

of any description. You might as well take a potato masher and endeavor to murder a medicine ball for all the benefit you will get from it

A GOOD ARM EXERCISE IN WHICH EITHER ELBOW MAY BE USED.
(Fig. 8.)

A simple one arm exercise, which every beginner will particularly appreciate, is shown in Fig. 9. To execute this stroke you must necessarily stand closer to the bag than in the right and left lead positions. Stand with the feet from six to twelve inches apart and on the same line. Raise, say, the right elbow, and strike the bag in the middle with its point. As the bag rebounds, strike it again and again. At first the movement will be somewhat tiring, but not for long. When you have become proficient with the right elbow, try the left. You will need more practice than with the right, to "educate" the left arm, unless you happen to be left handed, like a well-known humorist who once said that he was "only half right." After a week or two you will be considerably surprised at the power you will find yourself capable of putting into one of these elbow blows.

After you have become adept in using your elbows singly you may then alternate them, just as I told you to do with the right and left leads.

THE LEFT HAND HOOK.
(Fig. 9.)

Hooks are very valuable blows. They are used frequently with decisive effect by boxers. They are delivered at close range and therefore should have great speed. Stand with the feet about fourteen inches apart and advance the left foot about six inches before the right. Bend the elbow sharply. Raise the fist to a point on a line with the left hip and pivoting on the ball of the left foot, keeping the right foot steady, as a brace, shoot the fist to the middle of the bag as swiftly as possible. Instantly bring the fist back and repeat. Hold the right fist in front of the breast or chin as a means of defence. The bag will be

FIG. 14—RIGHT HAND SWING AS IT HITS THE BAG.

sent in a slanting direction. The right hook should also be developed. It is delivered exactly after the fashion of the left hook. Put somewhat of an upward heave of the shoulder in this blow. As the fist lands, the elbow should not be entirely straightened. It should be bent at an angle of about fifteen degrees.

ALTERNATING SHORT RIGHT AND LEFT HOOKS.
(Fig. 10.)

Stand with the feet about sixteen inches apart and on a line with each other. Hold the shoulders and head well back. Raise the arms, with the elbows bent, so that the hands are even in height with the middle of the bag and each being about twelve inches away from it. Hit the bag in the centre with first one fist and then the other. Permit the bag to rebound but once after being hit. The exercise involved in this combination blow is unsurpassed for the shoulders, chest and arms. You will be forced to bend your wrist downward to some extent as you hit the bag in this movement. Do not encourage this tendeney.

AN UPPERCUT WITH THE RIGHT HAND, AND UPPER CUTS IN GENERAL.
(Fig. 11.)

The uppercut resembles the hook. In the former, however, the fist is carried upward from a position closer to the body than is the case with the latter.

Uppercuts should not be allowed to swing too wide. When about to execute an uppercut stand about fourteen inches back from the bag. Bend the arm at an angle of about ninety degrees, and bring the fist up forcibly from a point below the hip and somewhat to the rear. Do not let the hand go far from the body until it is opposite the chest. In the right uppercut, as you carry your hand forward and upward to deliver the blow, RISE ON THE TOES OF THE RIGHT FOOT, as I have done in illustration No. 11. DO NOT FAIL TO HEED

FIG. 15—HALF SWING WITH LEFT HAND.

THIS INSTRUCTION, for by coming up on your toes you can put double the force into the stroke—enough in many cases to lift a man of your own weight off his feet. Keep the left leg firm. You must use it to steady yourself, to aid you to gauge distance accurately. When delivering a left uppercut, follow the example of the golfer as he supports himself on his right leg when he swings or drives.

HALF UPPERCUT WITH THE LEFT HAND.
(Fig. 12.)

The half uppercut, as the title of the blow signifies, lacks the full power or field of action held by the full uppercut. The left half uppercut should start from slightly above and to the front of the left hip bone. The right half uppercut is executed vice versa. In other respects these blows are similar to the right and left uppercuts. The left half uppercut is used more frequently than that with the right. While delivering a stroke of this sort with the left, hold the right across the front of the body, as I have done in illustration No. 12. Rise and pivot on the ball of the right foot, and in the right half uppercut do likewise with the left foot.

SWINGS AND HOW TO DELIVER THEM EFFECTIVELY.

Swings, as is of course well known, are blows of terrific force. When they take effect something is certain to happen. As these blows have a long distance to travel, they must be executed quickly to be of value. Fifteen minutes practice with a bag every day for two or three weeks will enable you to swing in splendid fashion. You will be surprised at the number of times you will be able to land a swing on an actual opponent when you have perfected it.

In swinging at the punching bag endeavor to be as accurate as possible. A wild swing is always a menace to the man delivering it, for it leaves him, what boxers would describe, as "wide open." Then, too, if you lunge wildly at the bag you will possibly miss it altogether, and thus lose your balance.

FIG. 16—HALF SWING WITH RIGHT HAND.

When delivering a full swing always remember to guard yourself with the disengaged hand. Consider the bag to be a wary opponent who will at the first opportunity take advantage of any opening that offers. By using your imagination in this way, you will find increased interest attached to your bag punching operations. Naturally the violence of swings prevents you from repeating the blow until the bag has rebounded several times. Perhaps you may be forced to let it go back and forth four or five times before duplicating the stroke.

THE FULL SWING WITH THE RIGHT HAND.

(Fig.13.)

To deliver a full right hand swing take the conventional sparring position, with the left foot advanced. Gauge accurately the location of the bag, and its distance from your right fist, which should be tightly clinched and held in front of the breast bone.

Hold the point of the chin well in, and after deciding on just what part of the bag you will strike—preferably as close to its centre as possible—step in swiftly with the right foot, advancing it far enough to place you within easy striking distance of the bag. Bring up the left fist to guard, as directed, and carrying the right fist well back and low, swing your right powerfully, in a half circle, landing on the bag with the impulse of the muscles of the arm, shoulders and back, combined with the impetus of your advance. Incline your head to the left. Hold your left fist in front of your face, as you would if an opponent blocked your right swing with his left and countered with a right swing, a hook or a jab. Do not throw the weight of your body forward past your right foot. If you do so, you will not be capable of springing out of harm's way, or in position to repeat the blow without delay.

Set yourself firmly in delivering swings. I would suggest that you do not practice swings continuously for too long a time. Try them say for five minutes, then rest a few minutes, and begin

FIG. 17—RIGHT SHIFT AND BLOCKING RETURN

again. Three five-minute periods a day are sufficient. My reason for so advising you lies in the fact that these blows are tiring, and you will readily admit that when a man is fatigued he cannot maintain good form and accuracy.

After learning the right swing practice the left. Advance the left foot instead of the right, and defend yourself with your right hand, the while inclining your head and chest to the right. Left swings usually start from a higher point than do right swings, because the left shoulder is generally lifted above the right. The left swing is neither so powerful nor so important a blow, still it is used the more frequently because it is easier to deliver. When you have become adept at both swings alternate them, stepping back into the sparring position after each stroke.

THE PUNCHER'S POSITION AS HE STRIKES THE BAG WITH A RIGHT HAND SWING.

(Fig. 14.)

In illustration, Fig. 14, I exhibit the correct pose for the bag puncher as he delivers a right hand swing. Observe closely the poise of the body and how I have placed my feet. In actual fighting I would incline to the left to a greater extent than shown in the photo. Be careful to clench your fist correctly by all means for in a heavy swing even the slightest twist may result in painful injury. At the moment your hand hits the bag you should be at the extreme height of your speed. Concentrate every iota of energy into the blow and release it at the exact instant that your hand comes in contact with the leather.

CONCERNING HALF SWINGS.

Half swings are well described by their name. They might be termed full swings with their wings clipped. A half swing starts from a point about half way between the starting and finishing places of a complete swing.

In the ring a half swing seldom if ever results in a knockout, therefore you may readily perceive that it lacks the force of

FIG. 18—THE OVERHAND—SHOULD NEVER BE USED.

the full swing, which is very true. It is used principally to temporarily bewilder a man and cause him if possible to leave an opening for a decisive punch.

A HALF SWING WITH THE LEFT HAND.
(Fig. 15.)

In the delivery of a left hand half swing stand about a foot closer to the bag than you would in executing a full swing. Take the sparring position, holding the right fist in front of the chest or chin. Step in, and start your left fist from a point about a foot straight out to the left of your left hip. Swing it forward and upward in a half circle, hitting the bag with face of your clenched knuckles. Step, or better, jump back into your original position, and when the bag's rebounds have slowed somewhat, step forward and strike it again. The bag will bounce in a slanting direction, but it will not vary its course if you hit · it in the same spot each time.

A HALF SWING WITH THE RIGHT HAND.
(Fig. 16.)

Reverse the instructions regarding the left half swing when executing the same sort of a blow with the right hand. The right half swing is more forcible than the left. Swing the body with the arm, turning at the waist, and do not overreach yourself.

THE SHIFT.

The shift is a movement that may be said to have received recognition in comparatively recent years. Fighters, old-time and modern, have used variations of it, but those of the latter days are responsible for its development to its highest form. Bob Fitzsimmons has frequently used shifts with "striking" effect.

A shift, briefly described, is a feint, combined with a sudden changing, or shifting of position to either side, at the same time landing a blow. The impetus gained by the advancement of the

FIG. 19—ANOTHER BLOW TO BE AVOIDED—RIGHT HAND UPPERCUT.

body makes the stroke a powerful one. A wide swing, a half swing, a hook or a half hook, etc., may be feinted to aid in the execution of a shift, two steps forward are usually taken.

THE SHIFT TO THE RIGHT AND THE POSITION FOR BLOCKING A RETURN.

(Fig. 17.)

There are two shifts, the left and the right. I will describe the shift to the right from which that to the left can easily be learned. To shift to the right, stand before the bag in the sparring pose, and not too close to it. Step forward briskly with the right foot, feinting a swing, or a hook, etc., with your right hand take another swift forward step, this time with your left foot and, bringing your right fist back to guard your face, swerve toward the right, bending somewhat, and as you set yourself on your left foot, land heavily on the bag with your left hand. Here is another of the blows in which the forward rush of the body lends crushing force. As the fist hits the bag, your body should lean to the right so that an imaginary opponent could not counter with his left to any advantage.

In shifting to the left, feint with the left hand, advance first the left foot, then the right, and bending the body to the left, land on the bag with your right fist, guarding yourself with your left.

THE OVERHAND SWING—NEVER USE IT IN PUNCHING THE BAG.

(Fig. 18.)

Do not make use of the overhand swing in bag punching. This blow is an exaggerated chop and serves to no good purpose, except in some phases of boxing. It gives a twang to the elbow that may result in a strain or a break, too. The stroke is awkward to deliver, and also makes difficult the landing of the fist squarely.

FIG. 20—RIGHT ELBOW EXERCISE.

THE RIGHT HAND UPPERCUT—THIS BLOW ALSO SHOULD BE AVOIDED.

(Fig. 19.)

Never use the right hand uppercut in manipulating the bag. You will but develop an improper and weak delivery of this important blow. The best method of learning it is to practice it with a companion or a sparring partner, and using boxing gloves.

_____

ELBOW EXERCISES.

Exercises with the elbows interject a new element of interest into the art of punching the bag. The elbows can be used singly, doubly, or in combination with the hands and even the head. These movements are particularly efficacious in, and recommended for, the development and raising of the shoulders. Athletic experts have devised dumbbell and Indian club maneuvers, which they term "shoulder raisers." Never, in all my experience, have I heard any gymnasium director or physical culturist speak of the punching bag in this especial connection, yet I unhesitatingly pronounce it to provide, in the elbow exercises, the best "shoulder raisers" in existence.

RIGHT, LEFT AND ALTERNATE ELBOW EXERCISES. THE RIGHT ELBOW.

(Fig. 20.)

The manipulation of the right elbow alone is done as follows: Stand close to the bag and to the left of it with the feet about two feet apart, clinch the right fist tightly and raising that elbow, strike the bag in the middle, or just below this point. To make the elbow as sharp as possible, bring the hand up and in, holding it close to your right breast. Strike the bag again on its first rebound, and keep it going rapidly. You can vary this exercise by hitting the bag with all your might and letting it rebound two or three times before again striking it. Another variation is the hitting of the elusive ball with either side of the elbow

FIG. 21—LEFT ELBOW EXERCISE.

alternately sending it to the right with the under or inner side and to the left with the upper or outer side. This last movement is merely a little trick, pretty to watch and hear, but of no especial value.

THE LEFT ELBOW.

(Fig. 21.)

Use the left elbow just as I have outlined the manipulation of the right, sending the bag of course to the left. The variations are the same for the left. Stand to the right of the ball, only about a foot, however, when hitting with the left elbow.

ALTERNATE ELBOW MOVEMENTS.

After you are an accomplished puncher with both elbows, try alternating them. Stand almost directly under the ball, and so that when still, it hangs with its middle opposite your nose. Clench both fists, hold them up close to your chest, and hit first with the right elbow, then with the left. There will be two bounces between each stroke. Hit the bag with the right elbow to the right side of the apparatus; as it comes back, let it go across to and rebound from the left side, when you then hit it with the left elbow. As you alternate upward and downward they will resemble the walking beam of one of the old Mississippi packets, but "don't you care."

TATTOOS.

A tattoo is a mode of striking a bag so that it will rebound rapidly, and causing the sound of the bouncing to be continuous and have rhythm. Many kinds of tattoos are at the command of the puncher. They are both simple and complex tattoos; in the latter, several different parts of the body being brought into play.

In order to obtain the desired results, tattoos should be executed with dash and accuracy. The blows should be as uniform as possible in power unless certain strokes are to be accentuated in order to produce a studied effect.

One of the chief values of strokes coming under this head

FIG. 22—TATTOO WITH BOTH HANDS.

Is the fact that they encourage, indeed almost invariably demand, the alternate use of at least both hands, and frequently call into action the elbows and sometimes even the head. Thus it will plainly be seen that tattoos develop a two-handed hitter, a kind of a man known among pugilists as a "two handed fighter." Also they help a man to strike with lightning like rapidity, and teach him to maintain a cool head under bewildering circumstances. Not the least among the attributes of tattoos is their tendency to quicken the eye and the brain.

TATTOO IN WHICH TWO HANDS ALONE ARE USED.
(Fig. 22.)

A popular form of tattoo is executed by standing directly in front of the bag, close to it, and hitting out straight in front, hitting the ball alternately with either hand. Keep the ball going rapidly, striking it squarely with the fist. Another tattoo somewhat similar to the foregoing is done as follows:

Stand close to the bag and send it to the left with a short right hook. Do so again on the first rebound and repeat the maneuver a certain number of times. After using the right fist, alternate with the left, striking the same number of blows as with the right. If you choose you may begin by striking a single blow with the right, and then one with the left, inserting a series of consecutive right or left blows whenever you wish. The tattoo I spoke of in the opening sentence of this section was probably the foundation of all other strokes of this sort.

A TATTOO WITH ELBOW AND HAND.
(Fig. 23.)

Stand slightly to the right of the bag and place the right foot in front of the left. Raise the right elbow and hit the bag so that it bounds forward and to the right in a slanting direction. Follow quickly with the left fist, on the first rebound. Alternate elbow and fist as swiftly as possible. After learning this combination of the right elbow and right fist, develop the use of the left elbow and the right fist.

~ FIG. 23—TATTOO WITH ELBOWS AND HANDS.

HOW TO BEAT A TATTOO WITH BOTH ELBOWS AND BOTH HANDS.

The elbows add complications to more alvanced forms of the tattoo. An effective manner of punching the bag with hands and elbows, and which appears to be three times more difficult than really is the case, I will now make known to you. Stand close to the bag, separating the feet, sideways, by about twenty inches. Neither one should project beyond the other. Hit the bag, say, with the left elbow, as it rebounds meet it with the right fist. On the next rebound let it swing to the opposite (the right) side of the apparatus. Meet the first rebound with the right elbow, the second with the left fist. On the next rebound, let the bag swing to the left side, when the same strokes are repeated, etc.

Tattoos seem possibly of infinite variation. To add another to your list, insert a back hand blow, or better, tap, in the combination blow I have just described. By so doing you will have mastered what we might term a "triple tattoo." When you have hit the bag to the left with the left elbow, meet the first rebound with a tap from the back of the left hand. Save the right fist for the second rebound. As the bag comes back from the right side the first time, jab it with the right elbow, following with the back (or knuckles) of the right hand on the second bounce, the left hand then taking effect on the next rebound. The order of these blows will be as follows: Left elbow, back of left fist, right hand—these punches sending the bag to the left; to the right—right elbow, back of right fist, left hand.

PUNCHING THE BAG BY MEANS OF THE HEAD, FRONT AND BACK.

(Fig. 24.)

The head may play an important part in bag punching. It can be used alone in various ways, and also in combination. By punching or butting the bag with the head, you will greatly

FIG. 24—HITTING THE BAG WITH HEAD—FRONT AND BACK.

strengthen the muscles of the neck and partly those of the shoulders. In addition you will accustom yourself to receiving blows on the head to such an extent that when you encounter them in boxing they will be robbed of their intended effect to some degree. Therefore head punching may be said to serve a twofold purpose.

Probably the best head movement is performed by standing directly under the bag and alternating forward and backward blows, in the first projecting the bag by means of butts with the forehead, and in the latter hitting it with the back of the head. When you butt the bag forward, let it rebound to the back of the apparatus. Then on its next rebound (the first from the rear) force it back again, and permit it to swing across to the forward side of the apparatus, so that it will rebound for another forehead blow. Try this maneuver a few times at first and gradually increase the number. Of course you should not wish to develop the neck to a marked extent. A neck with too much muscle is thick and unsightly, and is an undesirable possession for a man who is not a heavyweight pugilist of the slugging, unscientific school.

You can also divert yourself by using either the forehead or the back head movement individually. The first named butt develops the throat muscles particularly; the back head blow acts principally on the muscles extending between the back of the head and the shoulders.

HITTING (OR BUTTING) THE BAG WITH THE SIDES OF THE HEAD.

(Fig. 25.)

To develop the muscles of the sides of the neck and the tops of the shoulders, stand under the bag and propel it first to the left with the left side of the head, then to the right with the right side, striking in both cases with the upper part of the head's side, if possible, well above the ears.

This blow, enlarging and strengthening the muscles of the sides of the neck, completes the list of best known head ma

FIG. 25—HITTING THE BAG WITH SIDES OF THE HEAD

neuvers. It is practically needless to mention the fact that either side of the head may be used alone, just as in the case of the front and back blows. Do not try to produce any sort of a tattoo effect with the head, unless it is used in combination with the hands and the elbows, or both. The excessively rapid movement, or jerking, of the head is certain to induce dizziness and resultant discomfiture and inaccuracy.

In all head blows that I have described and portrayed in the illustrations, keep the feet well apart so as to form a brace. Unless you steady yourself in this manner you are absolutely sure to lose your balance.

THE CORRECT METHOD OF ALLOWING THE BAG TO SWING PAST THE HEAD.

(Fig. 26.)

Whenever it becomes necessary to let the bag swing past the head, do not drop, or squat, awkwardly under it. Ducking, of course, is permissible, and indeed advocated under certain circumstances. For ordinary purposes, however, keep the body erect, leaning forward a trifle, and inclining the shoulders (bending at the waist) and head to either side. Thus the bag will swing past your cheek. When leading with your left hand, invariably incline to the right. By so doing you would place yourself out of harm's way to some extent in a boxing match. A right hand lead should be accompanied, or better followed, by an inclination to the left. Rise on the ball of the right foot as you incline to the left, keeping both legs straight (with stiffened knees). Come upon the ball of left foot in leaning to the right.

Turn your face slightly away from the bag as it swings past your head, keeping your eyes on the bag however.

DO NOT DROP BOTH YOUR HANDS TO YOUR SIDES AT ANY TIME.

(Fig. 27.)

Always be careful to keep your hands, whether partly opened

FIG. 26—CORRECT WAY TO LET THE BAG PASS THE HEAD.

or clinched, raised as a possible means of protection. Never, at any rate, drop your hands and remain standing upright in the orbit of the bag. If you do, you are very likely to receive a painful blow in the face from the bounding bag, which I freely confess is no respecter of persons. A boxer who would drop both hands in the ring would meet with a sad and untimely end, therefore do not contract the habit in punching the bag. Remember that for the time being the bag is an opponent, and one that demands the respect of its antagonists. He who takes liberties with the punching bag will one day do the same with a real, live member of the fistic brotherhood, and may I be spared the task of writing a description of the obsequies.

THE INCORRECT METHOD OF AVOIDING THE BAG WHILE IT IS REBOUNDING.

(Fig. 28.)

In this pose I illustrate what not to do when the bag swings across from one side of the apparatus to the other. In addition to the awkwardness of your position and its pernicious effect, which I described in detail when referring to photo No. 26, the bag will oftentimes strike the top of your head in its passage, thus throwing it out of its natural course, or stopping its progress entirely.

———

THREE SIMPLE WAYS IN WHICH THE BAG MAY BE MANIPULATED.

Frequently a bag puncher wearies of the regularly prescribed blows, and takes a fancy to use an easy blow or two merely as a diversion to fill this need. I will now describe three strokes, A, B and C, that are as simple as can be desired.

A—(Fig. 29.)

Stand with the left foot advanced, the body slanting toward the bag. Strike with the left hand, sending the ball straight out in front. Hit it again with the left on the first rebound, and repeat the blow as many times as you like.

FIG. 27—DO NOT DROP YOUR HANDS TO YOUR SIDES AT ANY TIME.

B—(Fig. 30.)

Stand facing the bag almost squarely, possibly advancing the right foot a trifle. Guard yourself with your left, and hit the bag in the same manner as I directed you to do with left in the punch immediately preceding this.

C—(Fig. 31.)

With the legs apart, stand about twenty inches away from the bag and strike it with short hooks, alternating the hands. Put the swing and weight of the whole body into these punches. Strike the bag as it is about to pass your face in its rebounds.

Fig. 28—NEVER DUCK THE BAG THIS WAY.

A FEW WORDS REGARDING COMPETITIONS, EXHIBITIONS, ETC.

The bag puncher that educates himself with the idea in view that he will some day participate in contests against other performers, or will use his ability for exhibition purposes, must pursue a course differing from that of he who exercises for physical betterment only. The man with future competition in view should have three words to guide him at all times. They are accuracy, rapidity, and originality. Of the value and need of the first and second qualities I have already spoken in various of the foregoing pages. Concerning originality, I would say that every intelligent puncher of the bag can, if he but give the matter a little time and thought, develop new maneuvers, or at least, novel variations of old ones. A punch or series of punches somewhat out of the ordinary, and well executed, invariably has a favorable effect on judges.

Do not, by any means, permit yourself to become nervous, that is, unduly so, or disturbed in any way, during a contest or an exhibition. Weakness of this sort will put you "off your feed," and cause you to perform poorly. The deviation of a half inch, sometimes, in a punch, will throw you out of your stroke, and thus ruin the effect of an entire performance.

The exhibitor and the competitor, in addition, should always have and use his own private apparatus. All the prominent punchers own their own bags, framework, etc., and in becoming accustomed to them, are capable of better work than on an apparatus open to general use.

Make a point, too, of appearing in contests of any description in a neat, sightly, unencumbersome costume. Wear a sleeveless jersey if you would command the free use of your arms.

Do not attempt blows that are unreasonably fantastic. Fancy bag punching, of course, is a very admirable form of diversion, but there is a difference between fancy bag manipulation and

FIG. 29—AN EASY METHOD (SEE PAGE 53—A).

impracticable strokes that confuse in your mind whatever of merit you may already have learned. The practical bag puncher is one who does not waste time on exercises that are intensely intricate and that develops no particular muscles. He is also a person who, as a rule, can readily explain in accurate detail the blows he has mastered.

Do not punch the bag in a mechanical, monotonous sort of manner. Have a clearly defined reason for every move. Study the principles of cause and effect as applied to the puncher's realm of activity. There are bag punchers of my acquaintance that have more than ordinary control of the bounding, bouncing ball. They can interest and amuse even some of the most eritical experts. Yet, these selfsame individuals could not, for a full grown fortune, analyze any but the more simple blows. They know what they do, and when they do it, but as for how and why, well, that is a different matter. They are visionary, impractical folk, who will never advance beyond a certain point. After learning to execute a certain blow with one hand, repeat it with the other, as I directed in many of the preceding paragraphs relating to individual blows. Learn to perform the blow backward, if possible, and by so doing you will understand it the better. Every punch is made up of separate parts. In combination blows they are multiplied. Learn to know these component movements when you see them.

GOOD FORM AND HOW IT AFFECTS THE BAG PUNCHER.

How often we hear the term, "good form." In every branch of athletics it is applied in various ways, in every day life it comes into play, and in fact, every imaginable phase of existence the expression has its office. Good form is a merging under one head of good taste, observance of custom, propriety, and a general gracefulness of carriage and manner. The bag puncher who is in "good form" believes in being gentlemanly under all circumstances and in conforming to such regulations as govern his place of exercise. If in a gymnasium he will cease work after a period, to permit some other aspirant to practice. He will

FIG. 30—ANOTHER EASY METHOD (See Page 55—B).

not belabor the bag with powerful blows that make terrific noise, when people near find such interruption unpleasant, and he will not boast of superior accomplishment to such an extent that hearers will consider him a "blow hard" and an unmitigated bore. Let someone else sound your praises if you deserve them. The "good form" puncher is also one who gives careful attention to his dress. He is neat and trim, a pleasure to the eye.

In actual punching good form consists in maintaining absolute correctness in delivering strokes. The pose of the body will be one of ease. An idle hand or arm will be held in a position in harmony with the punch under consideration. Elbows will not project to the side unless they should. Knees will bend only at the proper intervals. The back and shoulders will be held erect when required. In fact, the smallest evidence of carelessness, or slouchiness will detract from what constitutes this highly to be desired ensemble of correctness—good form.

FIG. 81—SHORT RIGHT AND LEFT HOOKS (See Page 55—C).

"FIGHTING THE BAG"

AN ATTRACTIVE, HYGIENIC AND STRENUOUS FORM OF DIVERSION
WITH THE PUNCHING APPARATUS.

When a man has obtained what might be termed a "working knowledge" of bag punching, he may then indulge in an extremely fascinating and at the same time body-improving interchange of blows. The particular feature I have in mind is what pugilists call "fighting the bag."

In fighting a punching bag you conduct yourself exactly as you would if pitted against a boxer in the ring. You lead varied blows, blocking, ducking, and sidestepping the bag in its rebounds, and following up your leads with additional punches. Even a momentary consideration of this scheme will show the reader that striking (I do not use this word in the sense of a pun) possibilities exist in it. You can form endless variations, bringing every imaginable sort of a blow into play, in widely differing combinations. Ten minutes' practice twice a day in fighting the bag will produce wonderful advancement in your ability in the course of a month, and moreover, you will thus place at your command a highly attractive means for entertaining your friends, and for displaying your powers in exhibitions.

The average bag puncher pays little if any attention to fighting the bag, except with a succession of blows of the same description, or by repeating indefinitely the same punch. He thereby makes a mistake, which I sincerely trust the readers of this book will not imitate.

The seeming lack of system which attends the fighting of the bag in true pugilistic fashion does not necessarily offer an excuse for a puncher to deteriorate in form. While it is true that the use of a variety of blows in quick succession naturally tends to take the finish and accuracy from a man's work, yet you will find that by keeping your mind intently on what you are doing, and by beginning slowly, gradually warming up to the climax, you will be enabled to maintain an acceptable degree of meritorious and uniformly effective execution.

Of course I might continue under this subject and outline certain combinations of blows that I have used to advantage in fighting the spheroid. The best plan, however, will be to omit doing this, and thus make each individual puncher responsible for his own system, in this case. Originality will thus receive needed encouragement.

ALWAYS PRESERVE YOUR BALANCE.

While in the previous pages of this book I have occasionally mentioned the subject of balance, I wish to take this opportunity to consider it more fully. You should always bear in mind that the boxer who becomes easily unbalanced is one whose finish is approaching with fateful rapidity, and determine that you will never develop this weakness in punching the ball.

Whenever you strike be sure that your feet are so placed that either one or both will effectively brace your body as your hand and arm reach the outward limit of a punch, or as you lunge forward with the head and chest. In ducking, shifting and sidestepping, too, balance should receive unstinted consideration.

Balance, and by this I mean perfect balance, is as important to the puncher as a rudder is to a ship. If you deliver a blow and wobble on your legs like a weak-kneed old victim of dipsomania, you will present an inspiring sight, won't you? Spectators will be apt to remark "Huh, that fellow punch the bag; why, he hasn't learned how to stand yet."

Faulty balance is generally the result of either of two things, wild, cyclonic blows, and an improper position of the feet. Do not swing your arms wildly, because, in addition to throwing yourself out of balance, you are also left wide open for what in boxing would be a return blow; never hold your feet too close together. You will become unsteady and will resemble a tin soldier if you do. At the same time, always bear in mind that the height of awkwardness is shown by spreading your feet too far apart. There is a happy medium. Find it, and do not disregard it.

VALUE OF GAUGING DISTANCE

Hundreds of athletically inclined young men who would other wise develop into successful bag punchers and boxers are distinct failures because of their inability to gauge distance. The winning boxer is always a good judge of distance; bag punchers devoid of this attribute which, in fistiana might well be termed the sixth sense, never graduate from the novice class.

Gauging distance is, in bag punching, the act of estimating to a nicety the amount of space through which your fist must travel in order to hit the ball on a certain spot, and also of calculating accurately the direction the bag is swinging in, or the position or location in which it will be when your fist meets it. A sharp, quick eye and a keen, analytical mind are required.

As the ball bounds into position for your blow, gauge the distance, measuring in your mind the length of your reach and determining whether or not you will bend your body forward during the punch. Then shoot your hand out, completing the stroke, and maintaining your balance. Balance and distance gauging are the twin brothers of boxing and ball pounding. Each depends on, and works in harmony (at least so they should), with the other.

The object of distance gauging is to enable you to deliver a blow so that it will strike the objective point at the one moment when all the influences concerned are working together, are concentrated. The impetus of the body, the swing of the arm, the final compressing of the fist and the defence with the free arm and hand, should all be combined at the same instant, and it is at this psychological moment that the punch should take effect.

Gauging distance, too, is of use in defensive, as well as in offensive work. An accurate estimate of the course of the bag's swing, or of its variations, and in boxing, a calculation of an opponent's length of reach under varying conditions, etc., etc., often enables one to avoid a return by a simple inclination of the head, or a slight bend backward. Under the same circumstances, the novice would probably have jumped desperately backward, or lunged clumsily to one side or the other.

FANCY BAG PUNCHING

BY GUS KELLER, OF NEW YORK, UNBEATEN AS THE WORLD'S CHAMPION
AMATEUR BAG PUNCHER, AND NOW HOLDER OF THE
WORLD'S PROFESSIONAL CHAMPIONSHIP.

Fancy bag punching is very different, in some respects, from the ordinary, and what might be named the practical mode of manipulating the bag. While the last-named branch of the sport is designed to develop boxing ability, and promote the strength of the body, the fancy or purely exhibition branch does not aid the boxer to so great an extent, being more than anything else a means of specializing the punching of the bag as a science in itself. Moreover, it develops agility and rapidity in the movement of the hands and arms rather than well developed muscles.

Exhibition punching requires arduous study, constant practice, in fact, everything that is meant by the expression, "unceasing devotion." A few days of idleness is as fatal to dexterity as a month of disuse would be to a pianist's fingers.

The intricacy of some of the punches will at first seem appalling. An analysis of them, however, will speedily dispel most of the clouds. It is my purpose in this article to explain a few of the most attractive blows, and which can be added to the athlete's repertoire without considerable difficulty.

The history of exhibition bag punching in this country does not carry one back a great many years. Like the practical branch utilized by boxers, it is of comparatively recent development. At the present time, actual competitions are few and far between. The experts are scattered over wide territory, living in different States, and as prizes offered by promoters are seldom worth traveling a long distance to contest for, interest in matches is not wildly aroused. For instance, during the last decade, national championship matches for fancy bag punchers have averaged less than one a year, and it is a pity that enthusiasm has not been stirred by people who could, if they would, put the pastime on a regularly organized basis. The offering of suitable prizes for contests to be held under reputable management

66

would result in returns that would be a genuine surprise to all concerned. There are hundreds of able punchers, who have spent years in perfecting themselves, who would gladly sign to ‚compete under favorable circumstances.

During these days fancy bag punchers in the professional division, find their principal revenue to be derived from vaudeville theatres and appearances at entertainments, club smokers, etc.

The variations to which exhibition punching is susceptible are innumerable. When the combinations with one bag have been exhausted, you may introduce two bags, then another, and again a fourth. These may be kept in motion with the use of the feet or knees, in addition to the hands, elbows and head, until the performer resembles a double-jointed jumping jack with the St. Vitus' dance throughout his entire system. In the illustrations to which I will refer in pages to follow, I will describe the simul taneous use of two and three bags.

Interesting and perhaps fascinating to watch, the operations of the fancy bag puncher are also entertaining to the ear. Musi cal effects of various descriptions can be produced, and it is really surprising to learn how much rhythm and expression can be made evident in the rebounding of the ball. Tunes familiar to the hearers, can readily be recognized. "Yankee Doodle" and other simple airs are possible of amusingly realistic reproduction.

The floor bag which I show in several illustrations, is my own idea and invention. It may be used alone, or in combination. I use it with two high bags, sometimes, and again with one. Also, as you will observe by examining the photos, I use in conjunction with another floor bag. One of the advantages of the floor bag is that it brings different muscles into action from those engaged by the best known sort. The back and legs receive exercise impossible to be had in the pounding of the bag suspended from a ceiling. The floor bag may be hit with the hands, the elbows, the knees or the feet, singly or in combination.

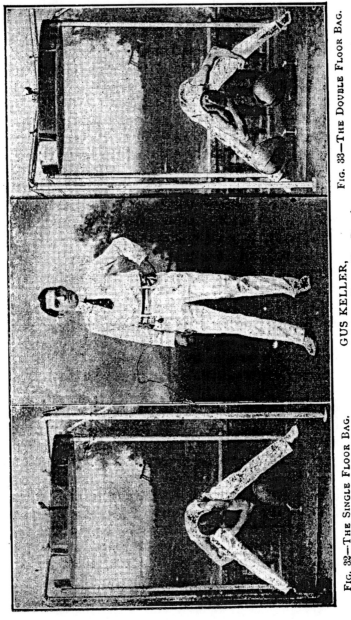

FIG. 32—THE SINGLE FLOOR BAG.　　GUS KELLER,　　FIG. 33—THE DOUBLE FLOOR BAG.

America's Cleverest Fancy Bag Puncher.

THE SINGLE FLOOR BAG—THE SIMPLEST OF FLOOR BAG EXERCISES.

The fundamental floor bag punch is the use of the single bag with both hands, driving it first to one side and then to the other, using the hands alternately. Stand about eighteen inches away from the bag, spread your feet as far apart as possible and straighten your legs, not allowing the knees to bend in the slightest degree. At first this position will strain the ligaments at the back of the knee joint and put considerable pressure on the muscles of the calves of your legs, but practice will overcome this discomfort and any others that may arise. Bend at the waist, and after putting the bag in motion by slapping it to either side with the opened palm, strike the bag say first with the right fist causing it to hit the floor at your left. Let it rebound to the right and as it rises from the floor send it to the right with your left. Do this about ten times on your first trial, increasing the number of punches as you progress. You can vary this maneuver by hitting the bag quite hard and letting it rebound two or three times before repeating your stroke with the other hand. The bag is held to the floor by means of a swivel and short piece of strong cord or rope

A SINGLE FLOOR BAG EXERCISE IN WHICH BOTH HANDS, ELBOWS, AND SOMETIMES THE HEAD ARE USED.

(Fig. 32.)

The floor bag movement I will now describe is somewhat involved, especially for those that have not yet entered the expert class. Let the cord to which the bag is fastened have about three inches play. This amount of slack, by the way, will be found ample for every floor bag exercise. After starting the ball in motion, hit it to the left side with the left elbow, meeting it on the first rebound with the back of the left fist. From the rebound, let the ball bounce over to the right side, and after striking it on the first rebound with the right elbow, return

FI . 34—SINGLE OVERHEAD AND KNEE   FIG. 35—PUNCHING TWO BAGS   FIG. 36—PUNCHING TWO OVERHEAD AND
BAGS.   SIMULTANEOUSLY   ONE FLOOR BAG SIMULTANEOUSLY

it to the same side with the back of the right fist.[1] After striking the bag with either of the back hand blows, you can meet the ensuing rebound with the head if you desire to insert a variation, returning the bag to the same side from which it rebounded, of course.

The head variation, however, should be tried only after the combination elbow and hand blow has been placed under perfect control.

The muscles of the back, shoulders and neck receive excellent exercise in the foregoing maneuver and such as they will get in no other form of bag punching. The hips will also be broadened and the strain which the position places on the ankles will strengthen those much neglected joints. Be sure to have your arms and shoulders absolutely free from all cumbersome clothing. Loosen your belt if you are accustomed to wearing it tight. Its pressure as you lean over will contract your abdomen and thus interfere with your breathing, and which is hindered by the position you are in, even under the most favorable circumstances. This pose in itself is extremely tiring, particularly at first, and therefore do not overtax your strength. Your blood may rush to your head somewhat until you are accustomed to the attitude, but practice will enable you to perform these blows without the slightest inconvenience.

PUNCHING TWO FLOOR BAGS AT ONCE.
(Fig. 33.)

I invented the floor bag about three years ago and afterward saw the possibility of using two of them simultaneously. In illustration No. 36 I show what is considered the easiest mode of operating the double floor bags. I place the balls about two feet apart and stand about eight inches back from them. The legs must be stretched as far apart as the human frame will permit. Keep the knees rigid. Strike the right hand ball with the right elbow; the left hand one with the left fist, making both of them swing to the right.

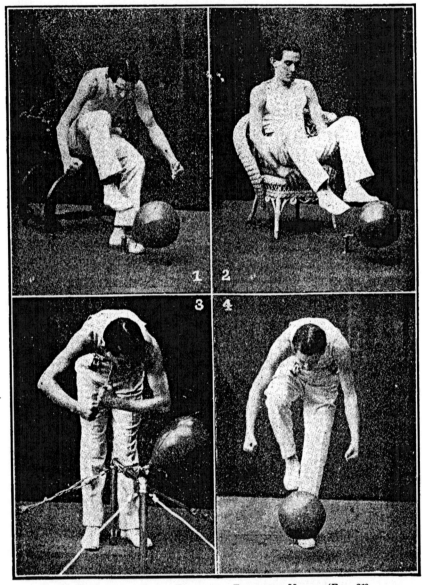

1—Punching a Floor Bag with Feet and Hands (Fig. 37).
2—Punching a Floor Bag with Soles of Feet (Fig. 38).
3—Rotary Bag, Using Elbows and Hands (Fig. 39).
4—Punching a Floor Bag with Feet and Hands (Fig. 40).

I do not let the double floor bags rebound far from the floor. I repeat the blows when they have risen but a few inches, say six or seven.

When tired of bunching the floor bags to the right, raise yourself and allow them to bounce over to the floor at the left. Now, on the first rebound, hit the left bag with the left elbow, instead of the left fist, as before, and punch the right hand spheroid with the right fist. If you like the idea you can alternate the direction of the bags from left to right, hitting them both in one direction, and then in the other.

Then too, the elbows may be introduced, using one elbow alone, on one ball, and an elbow and the back of the same fist, on the other, etc., etc.

MANIPULATING SIMULTANEOUSLY A SINGLE OVER HEAD BAG AND A KNEE BAG.

(Fig. 34.)

The possibilities for all around development in bag punching are admirably illustrated by the fact that the science permits of the operation of a bag with the hands at the same time the knees are keeping one in motion. During this exercise hardly a muscle in the entire body remains idle.

To perform this "stunt" put the floor bag directly under the overhead spheroid as shown in the photo (Fig. 34). Place your feet on either side of the floor bag with about six inches of space separating them. As your legs form an angle your knees will be about four inches apart.

Strike the overhead bag with the right fist, sending it to the left. At the instant your fist leaves the bag, bend sharply at the knees, hitting the lower bag with the bones of the legs just below the knee cap. As the upper bag comes back let it go to the right side, to which it is returned with the left fist on its first bound therefrom, not forgetting of course to continue bending at the knees to keep the lower ball in motion.

. After the upper bag is returned to the right with the left fist let the bag go to the left again, returning it to the same side with the left elbow, and to the same side again with the right fist. After this last blow, let the spheroid bound to the right side, where on the first rebound the right elbow returns it, only to be followed with another punch to the right with the left fist.

Continue the right elbow and left fist, and the left elbow and right fist combination blows in conjunction with the knee strokes for from four to eight minutes, unless you feel capable of prolonging the periods.

The variations of which the combined knee and overhead bags are possible are also of great number, several of which are possibly simpler than the foregoing.

With practice you can alternate the knees in using the floor bag. The right knee will slant the bag somewhat to the left, as the accurate hitting of the rounded surface of the knee is necessarily difficult. The left knee will incline it to the right. The amount of variation from a straight line, however, will not interfere materially with the performance of the blows, as the knees can be moved a trifle as they are bent, to counteract the deviation. It will not be advisable to alternate the knees while using the overhead bags at the same time as the complication of movement will render good results well nigh impossible.

Use the floor bag alone when alternating the knee strokes. If you hold your hands behind your back in this latter exercise, with the elbows projecting at either side, you will present an appearance better than that resulting from the holding of the hands as your sides, with the arms dangling loosely. In addition you will be aided in balancing yourself.

THE SIMULTANEOUS PUNCHING OF TWO BAGS OVER HEAD.

(Fig. 35.)

With two bags arranged overhead, as in illustration No. 33, you can use many variations. The exercise I have posed for is comparatively easy for any person with a keen eye and a "cool" head. Stand close to the bags with the left foot advanced before the right to a point directly under the bag that swings to your left. Face directly to the front, a trifle to the left of the right hand bag. Hit the left bag with the left elbow, at the same time striking the other with the outside of the clenched finger joints of your right fist. Do not bend your fist to hit with the broad face of the knuckles as you would in boxing, for you will lose time by so doing. Keep both bags bounding to your left, hitting each at exactly the same moment.

If you wish you may let them bounce over to the right side and then keep on returning them to that side hitting the right hand bag with the right elbow, and the left bag with the outside of the clenched finger joints of the left first. As the bags change over to the right, shift your position, advancing the right foot before the left, under the right hand bag. The puncher has a dull brain indeed who cannot invent at least a half dozen different ways in which to punch these two bags.

PUNCHING THREE BAGS AT ONCE—ONE FLOOR BAG AND TWO OVERHEAD.

(Fig. 36.)

Here we are confronted by a proposition that is more spectacular by far than difficult, even though appearances may indicate that an unusual amount of trouble and time should be expended in the perfecting of it. To learn the mode of punching three bags simultaneously, one at the knees and two to be manipulated by the hands, requires patience, and dogged determination, that's all.

Stand with the feet as close as possible to the swivel to which the knee bag is connected. This bag should be placed at a point in the floor exactly between the two upper bags. Hold the body perfectly erect between the two bags swinging from the top of the apparatus. Bring up the arms and bend the elbows at angles exactly corresponding, so that the hands will be close to the face, and about on a line with the chin or the middle of the bags. Strike outward with each fist, hitting each upper bag in its middle, and just after the blows land, bend sharply at the knees, striking the lower bag with both knees at the same time. Straighten your knees as quick as a flash so as to be in an upright position to repeat the first blows on the overhead bags. Repeat as many times as you feel you can stand comfortably.

Be very particular about the manner in which you hold your hands and in which you deliver your punches. Do not strike the upper bags with either the front or back of the fist. Hit them with the ends (sometimes called sides) of your clenched hands, the surface formed by the clenched little finger and the fleshy pad between the outside knuckle of this finger and the outside wrist bone, in short, the end (or side) opposite the thumb end (or side).

This mode of striking is not practical for other purposes. It is never used in boxing, but it is indispensable for certain blows in fancy bag punching. In this form of the sport, expediency must necessarily be given precedence above all other things. Whatever is practical for the fighter, but not expedient for the bag puncher, must be given but secondary consideration here, consequently the boxer is just as well, if not better, off if he leaves the exhibition end of the game out of his reckoning.

Variations are again possible in the three bag movements. I will not attempt to enumerate or describe them, however. It will be a very easy matter for any puncher to find them for himself. I will leave them to his ingenuity.

PUNCHING A FLOOR BAG (SITTING), USING THE FEET AND HANDS.

(Fig. 37.)

Sit on the extreme edge of a chair which has been placed about a foot back from the floor bag. Lean forward and start the ball bounding straight before you, hitting it alternately with the hands. When you have it bouncing in a satisfactory fashion, not too swiftly at this juncture, alternate the feet with the hands. Strike first with the right hand, then with the right foot; follow with the left hand and the left foot. Vary the exercise by changing the order in which you use your hands and feet and the number of times they are brought into play.

Balance yourself by touching the floor with the free foot between every blow. This maneuver is exceedingly fatiguing. A few minutes a day will suffice for even the most ambitious performers.

A single foot and a single hand can be used in combination to advantage. Do not at any stage bring the toe of either foot in contact with the bag. By so doing you will cause it to take a sudden jump that will throw you out of your stroke and destroy whatever rhythm you have succeeded in putting into the series of blows. Naturally a kick will give a bag more impetus than a careful tap with the sole of the foot.

SITTING AND OPERATING A FLOOR BAG WITH THE SOLES OF THE FEET.

(Fig. 38.)

On reading the heading of this section of the book, some of the uninitiated may imagine for a moment that the exercise to be considered is one that will give them a chance to rest. They will probably believe it to be a lazy man's task. Do not let any such idea linger in your brain for a hundredth part of a second. True, the bag puncher will now sit down to his work, but when he finishes, he is fully aware of the fact that there has been "something doing."

The calves of the legs and the ankles will be strengthened somewhat by this exercise in which the floor bag is kept in motion by the soles of the feet. Place a chair at such a distance from the bag that your feet will project about fourteen inches beyond the swivel when the legs are straightened. Draw up the knees, and while bracing the body with the hands grasping the seat of the chair. as in the illustration, hit the ball with one foot and then the other. The part of the sole of the shoe covering the ball and toes of the foot should come in contact with the bag.

Bend the ankles during the exercise. Do not let all the impulse come from the knees. Avoid hitting the bag with the heels. Brace your back firmly against the back of the chair. Throw your shoulders well to the rear. Hold your chin in and watch the bag closely. Very the movements by sometimes hitting the bag with a single foot continuously.

A BAG PUNCHING NOVELTY—THE ROTARY BAG, WITH WHICH THE ELBOWS AND THE HANDS, SINGLE OR IN COMBINATION, ARE USED.

(Fig. 39.)

The rotary bag makes necessary a new sort of apparatus, similar to that shown in illustration No. 41. However, on trying the innovation, experienced punchers will find themselves anxious indeed to expend the small sum required to procure it.

In the use of the rotary bag the hands alone, the elbows alone, or both hands and elbows can be brought into action in several combinations.

The rotary apparatus consists of three pieces of ordinary gas pipe joined as shown in the aforementioned illustration, and each of which should be about two feet long. Small wire cable or strong rope can be extended to four eyes fastened in the floor in the same manner as shown in the photo, form satisfactory "stays."

The bag is suspended from the middle of the top section of pipe—the cross piece. The cord to which it is attached is looped around the pipe, thus affording a connection permitting rapid rotation.

To punch the rotary bag start it going with the hand, say from left to right. It must not touch the floor. As the bag swings under the cross piece and upward to the right, meet it with the right fist. Hit is moderately at first. Let it spin around two or three times. Then meet it with the left fist, sending it whirling round and round in the opposite direction. Follow the left fist punch with a right elbow blow, and vice versa. You can let the bag swing around more than the three times or less, as you think best. Then again, you can punch it back and forth, using the hands alternately, without making use of the elbows, or you can let the elbows do all the work.

To those never having used a rotary bag, the illustration, of which these paragraphs are descriptive should be the subject of careful study.

STANDING AND KEEPING A FLOOR BAG IN MOTION WITH FEET AND HANDS.

(Fig. 40.)

To add another punch to the list of floor bag variations, stand with the feet directly against the swivel (on either side). Strike the bag first with the right fist, then with the ball of the right foot; then with the left foot, following with the left fist. To vary the movement, use first both hands, then both feet alternately.

Here again the muscles of the back and legs are given effective exercise. Care must be taken that the fists strike the bag as near its middle as possible. It is highly desirous that the spheroid be given as little slant in its rebounds as is consistent with fast work. Always make sure that the bag used in foot blows is well inflated. An unresponsive ball will destroy all chance of good results.

PUNCHING A FLOOR BAG WITH KNEES AND HANDS.

A movement somewhat similar to the preceding one is performed by keeping the ball (the floor ball) in motion with the hands and knees, instead of with the hands and feet. Place the feet close to, and on either side of the swivel. Stand erect and hit the bag with first one knee, then the other. Follow with using the hands alternately. Vary the pastime by hitting the bag different numbers of times consecutively with either hand or either foot, before alternating in this order for instance, or similar.to it:

Right hand, three times; left hand, three times; left knee, three times; right knee, three times.

If you choose, strike four or five consecutive blows before changing to the other hand or foot, instead of the three, or in preference to a single blow as first suggested.

SPALDING BOXING GLOVES
"CHAMPIONSHIP" STYLES

No. 118

No. 115

No. 116

No. 18N

"EXPERT" SPARRING AND FIGHTING STYLES

o. 118. 8-ounce. Highest grade made.
Set of four gloves, $8.00

o. 115. 5-ounce. Set of four gloves, 6.50

o. 116. 6-ounce. Set of four gloves, 7.00

No. 18N. Spalding "Navy Special" Championship Glove. Used by champions of the navy. Special "Sea Green" leather; furnished in 8-oz. only; padded laced wristband; patent palm lacing, patent palm grip. Set of four gloves, $6.00

No. 11

No. 9

No. 218

No. 12

o. 11. Corbett Pattern. Large 7-oz. model. Best quality brown leather, substantially made. Padded wristband; patent palm lacing; patent palm grip. Set of four gloves, $6.00
o. 9. 5-ounce Regulation. Special brown glove leather. Supplied in regular and large sizes. Padded wristband, special padded thumb, patent palm lacing and patent palm grip. Set of four gloves, $5.00

No. 218. Spalding "Club Special" Gloves. 8-ounce "Championship" model, full size. Good glove leather. Padded wrist, patent palm lacing, patent palm grip. Set of four gloves, $5.00
No. 12. Spalding "Member Special" Gloves. 8-ounce Corbett pattern, good size. Black glove leather trimmed with red leather. Padded wrist; special padded thumb; patent palm lacing, patent palm grip. Set of four gloves, $5.00

SPALDING BOXING GLOVES

No. 110

No. 110. Pupil's Double Wrist Pad. Large model. Best grade brown glove leather, additionally padded on the forearm and over the wrist to prevent that soreness which is one of the most discouraging features following a brisk lesson in the art of "blocking." Made after the suggestion of one of the most prominent athletic officials in this country. Patent palm grip and palm lacing. . Set of four gloves, $7.50
No. 200. Instructor's 10-ounce. Special thumb model. Best grade special treated boxing glove leather, extra heavily padded over the knuckles and with special large padded thumb to prevent injury to either instructor or pupil. The leather in this glove is particularly durable, and it does no get hard or ruff up when wet or subject to severe usage. Used by the instructor's in most of the large gymnasiums and .

No. 200

boxing schools and by many prominent pugilists in training. Lace extra far down for ver lation. Patent palm grip. . . . . Set of four gloves, $7.
No. 100. Same as No. 200, but of brown glove leather. . . . . Set of four gloves, 7.

All Spalding Boxing Gloves are hair filled.   No cotton or carpet flock is used.
STYLES FOR FRIENDLY BOUTS AND PRIVATE USE

No. 14   No. 15   No. 19   No. 21   No. 28

No. 14.   5-ounce Regulation. Brown glove leather. Special padded thumb, wrist and heel; patent palm lacing and palm grip. Used by some of the best organizations for their club contests.   . Set of four gloves $4.00
No. 15. 8-ounce Corbett Pattern. Special olive tanned leather; padded wristband; patent palm lacing; patent palm grip. The proper glove for friendly bouts and use at home.
            Set of four gloves, $4.50

No. 19. 7-ounce Corbett Pattern. Dark w color leather. Patent palm lacing.
            Set of four gloves, $4.
No. 21.   8-ounce Regular Pattern.   W color, with brown palm. Patent palm laci Padded cuffs.   . Set of four gloves, $3.
No. 28. 5-ounce Regulation Pattern. Red l ther, oak color palm; special padded thu padded wrist; patent palm lacing. Supplie regular and large sizes. Set of four gloves, $3

SPALDING BOXING GLOVES

MEN'S PRACTICE STYLES

No. 22. **Corbett Pattern.** Men's practice model.
Brown glove leather, with wine colored leather palm;
padded wrist; patent palm lacing.

Set of four gloves, **$3.00**

No. 23. **New Style Turned End Pattern.** Wine
colored leather, with brown palm; correctly padded,
and patent palm lacing. Set of four gloves, **$2.50**

No. 23N. Black leather, padded wrist; turned
end pattern. Comfortable and practical. Patent palm
lacing. . . . . Set of four gloves, **$2.25**

No. 24K. Style of No. 23, but slightly larger and
made with khaki palm. . Set of four gloves, **$2.00**

SPALDING YOUTHS' BOXING GLOVES

Spalding Youths' Boxing Gloves are made in exactly
the same manner and of similar material to the full
size gloves of our manufacture, and are warranted to
give satisfaction.

No. 45. **Youths' "Championship" Glove, Corbett
Pattern.** Best quality brown glove leather and extra
well finished. Double stitched; patent palm lacing;
patent palm grip. . . . Set of four gloves, **$3.50**

No. 40. **Youths' Size, Turned End Pattern.** Wine
colored leather, well padded. Patent palm grip;
patent palm lacing. . . Set of four gloves, **$3.00**

No. 25. **Youths' Size, Regular Pattern.** Soft tanned
leather, patent palm lacing. Set of four gloves, **$2.00**

No. 25K. Style of No. 25, but slightly larger and
made with khaki palm. . Set of four gloves, **$1.50**

No. 40

All Spalding Boxing Gloves are hair filled.

No cotton or carpet flock is used.

No. 22

No. 23N

Spalding Boxing Helmet

Complete protection for ears, nose
and eyes. Well ventilated.

Each, **$3.50**

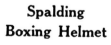

No. 45

No. 25

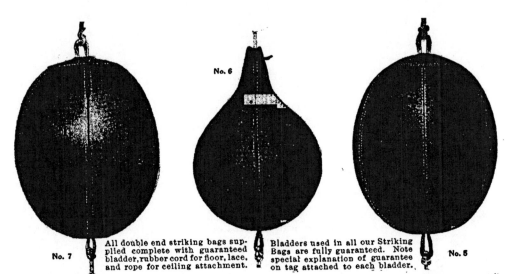

No. 6

All double end striking bags supplied complete with guaranteed bladder, rubber cord for floor, lace, and rope for ceiling attachment.

Bladders used in all our Striking Bags are fully guaranteed. Note special explanation of guarantee on tag attached to each bladder.

No. 7

No. 5

No. 7. Finest selected olive Napa tanned leather, workmanship same as "Fitzsimmons" Special No. 18. Double stitched, red welted seams. Extremely durable and lively. .. Each, $6.00

No. 6. Fine olive tanned leather cover, double stitched, red welted seams Extra well made throughout. . . Each, $5.00

No. 5. Regulation size; specially tanned brown glove leather cover, red welted seams, double stitched and substantially made. Each, $5.00

Elastic Floor Attachments for all Double End Bags
No. D. Best elastic cord. . . . . Each, 35c
No. E. Elastic cord. . . . . " 20c.

No. 4

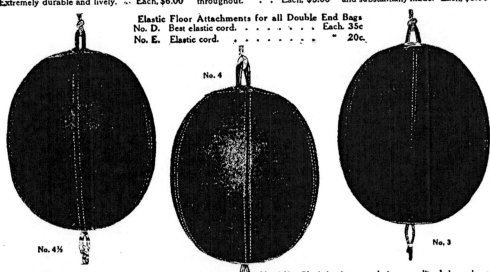

No. 4½

No. 3

No. 4½. Regulation size, wine colored leather, double stitched and red welted seams. . . . . . Each, $4.00
No. 4. Regulation size, tan colored leather cover, well made throughout, double stitched. . . . Each, $3.50
No. 3. Regulation size, substantial brown leather cover, reinforced and double stitched seams. . .. Each, $3.00

No. 3½. Black leather regulation size, lined throughout, red welted seams . . . . Each, $2.50
No. 2½. Regulation size, good quality dark olive tanned leather, lined throughout, red welted seams. . Each, $2.00
No. 2. Medium size, good colored sheepskin, lined throughou . . . . Each, $1.50

No. JJ

No. G.

No. 19

No. JJ. .Special training bag. Same as used by Champions both here and abroad, to get into condition for important contests. Leather is a special selection of brown calfskin, very smooth and particularly durable. . . . Each, **$10.00**

No. G. This is a heavy, durable gymnasium bag, suitable for all around exercise work and the strongest bag made. The cover is of heavy English grain leather, same as used in our best grade foot balls and basket balls and made in the same way. It will outlast two or three bags of any other make. With loop top. . . . . Each, **$9.00**

No. 19. Made of highest quality Patna kid, the lightest and strongest of leather. Sewed with linen thread, double stitched and red welted seams. Especially suited for exhibition work, and a very fast bag. . . . . Each, **$8.00**

No. 19S. Same material as No. 19, but furnished with special light bladder and weighs only 7½ ounces complete. The fastest bag made, but very strong and durable. . . . . Each, **$8.00**

No. 20

No. 20. Made of finest selected brown calfskin, with olive welted seams. A very fast and durable bag for all around use. . . . . Each, **$7.50**

No. 20G. Model of our popular No. 20 bag, but made of black horsehide. Very durable. . , . . Each, **$7.00**

No. 18. The "Fitzsimmons Special." Made of finest selected olive Napa tanned leather, extra well made, double stitched, red welted seams and reinforced throughout. For training purposes particularly this bag will be found extremely satisfactory in every respect. . . . Each, **$6.00**

The Bladders used in all our Striking Bags are fully guaranteed.

No. 18

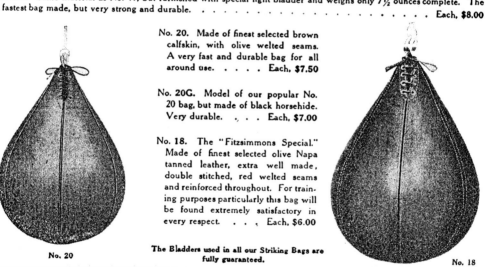

PRICES SUBJECT TO CHANGE WITHOUT NOTICE. For Canadian prices see special Canadian Catalogue

Bag punching is really a fascinating diversion, capable of so many combinations, that it is interesting alike to the young boy and the seasoned athlete. When its healthful advantages are considered it is remarkable that there are not more bags in use, especially where there are boys and girls who would not otherwise take sufficient exercise to keep them in good physical condition. The same is true of many business men who really could use a punching bag with benefit and very conveniently, where in many cases sufficient outdoor exercise is simply impossible.

No. 12. Olive tanned leather, specially selected; double stitched, red welted seams and reinforced throughout. Excellent for quick work. Each $5.00

No. 10. Specially tanned brown glove leather; double stitched, red welted seams and reinforced throughout. Very well made. .. .. Each, $4.00

No. 12

No. 10

Our single end striking bags are made with rope attachment carefully centered, making them the most certain in action of any. Laces on side at top, so that the bladder may be inflated without interfering with rope.

The Bladders used in all our Striking Bags are fully guaranteed.

No. 17

No. 16

No. 15½

No. 17. Fine craven tanned leather, well finished; double stitched, red welted seams, reinforced throughout. Each, $3.50
No. 16. Extra fine tan colored leather, full size and lined throughout. .. .. " 3.00
No. 15½. Black leather, full size and lined throughout; red welted seams. .. .. " 2.50

SPALDING SINGLE END STRIKING BAGS

Our single end bags are made with rope attachment carefully centered, making them the most certain in action of any. Laces on side at top, so that the bladder may be inflated without interfering with rope. Each bag is most carefully inspected and then packed complete in box with bladder, lace and rope.

No. 15. Made of olive tanned leather, full size and lined throughout; red welted seams. Each, $2.00

No. 14. Good quality colored sheepskin; lined throughout. . . . . Each, $1.50

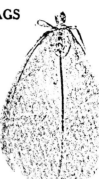

No. 15

No. 14

STRIKING BAG BLADDERS

BLADDERS

No. G. For No. G-Bag. Each, $1.75

No. OS. For any full size top stem bag. . Each, $1.25

No. 7. For No. 7 bag. " 1.00

No. 7P. For Nos. 20, 20G, 19, 19S and 18. . . . Each, 1.00

BLADDERS

No. 5. For Nos. 6, 5, 4 and 4½. Ea.,

No. 5P. For Nos. 17, 16, 12 and 1 Each, $

No. B. For Nos. 3½, 3, 2½ an bags. Each,

No. BP. For Nos. 15½, 15 and bags. Each,

SPALDING STRIKING BAG SWIVELS

No. 4

No. 4. A special swivel, made according to suggestions of experienced bag punchers, with features that overcome disadvantages of ordinary style. Rope can be changed instantly without interfering with any other part of swivel. . . Each, $1.50

No. 5. Nickel-plated swivel with removable socket for quickly suspending or removing bag without readjusting. . . . . Each, 75c.

No. 12. Ball and Socket Action. Fastens permanently to disk; nickel-plated. " 25c.

No. 5. Top View. Showing opening for rope, which is removable.

No. 5. Under V Showing nec swivel, which i tened permane

SPALDING BRASS INFLATERS

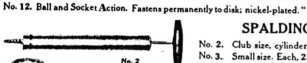

No. 2

No. 3

No. 2. Club size, cylinder 10½ inches. . . . . . . Each,

No. 3. Small size. Each, 25c.

SPALDING STRIKING BAG MITTS

Will protect the hands and are recommended for use with all Striking Bags

No. 1. Made of olive Napa leather and extra well padded; ventilated palm and spe elastic wrist in glove. . . . . Pair, $2

No. 2. Made of soft tanned leather, properly shaped and padded, substantially together. . . . . Pair, $1

No. 3. Made of soft tanned leather, padded and well made; also m in women's size. . . . . Pair, $

No. 4. Knuckle Mitt, well padded. . . . . "

No. 5. Knuckle Mitt, well padded. . . . . "

No. 1   No. 4   No. 5

Spalding "Moline" Disk

Combines adjustable feature of our popular Moline Platform with the practical utility of the solid disk.

No. 1D.
Moline Adjustable Disk, including No. 5 style striking bag swivel.
Each, **$20.00**
Bag is not included in above price.

No. 1D

Spalding "Moline" Platform

Adjustable in height, readily attached to any wall, and the side brackets so arranged that it touches three rows of studding. Neat in design and finish. Supplied with everything necessary for attaching to wall, and crated ready for shipment.

No. 1. Moline Platform.
Each, **$15.00**

Bag is not included in above price.

No. 1

No. PR
Patented April 19, 1904

Spalding Disk Platform

Can be put up in a very small space and taken down quickly when not in use by simply detaching the pipe fixture from the wall plate. The metal disk against which the bag strikes constitutes one of the best features ever incorporated in an arrangement of this character, rendering it almost noiseless and very quick in action. Combines an adjustable feature, making it possible for various members of family to use same disk.

No. PR. Spalding Disk Platform. Complete, *with special bag.* . . Each, **$8.00**
No. PR. Spalding Disk Platform. *Without bag.* . . . . " **5.00**

Unless otherwise specified on order, bag will be sent WITH platform.

Spalding Striking Bag Disks

A striking bag disk must be substantial if it is to be of use, and in the two styles, both adjustable and braced, which we list, this feature has not been neglected, while we have striven to put out a disk which is suitable for home use and moderate in prices.

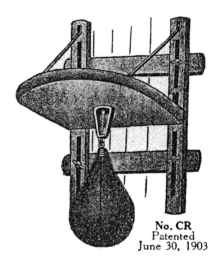

No. FR

R. Patent adjustable style. Complete, *out bag.* . . . . Each, **$8.00**

. Wall braced style. Complete, *with-bag.* . . . . Each, **$5.50**

No. CR
Patented
June 30, 1903

Spalding Adjustable Floor Disk

This style is what is generally called a "Floor Disk," because the heavy japanned pipe uprights and the steel guys are attached to the floor, but this one is superior to any similar style now on the market in that it combines with absolute rigidity the adjustable features so necessary in an article that is for home use, to make it suitable for various members of the family. Capable of three adjustments of two inches each or a total of 6 inches. Floor space required: 9 feet by 6 feet; height, 7 feet. Uprights placed 6 feet apart, allowing plenty of foot room.

No. **82F.** Spalding Adjustable Floor Disk, without bag or bag swivel. . . . . Each, **$25.00**

SPALDING
BASKET BALL SHOES

No. AB

No. **AB.** High cut. drab leather, Blucher cut; heavy red rubber suction soles, superior quality.
Pair, **$6.00**

No. **BBL.** Women's. High cut, light; black leather, good quality red rubber suction soles. Pair, **$5.00**

No. BBL

SPALDING GYMNASIUM SHOES

No. 15
Correct
Shoes for
Boxing

No. 166

No. 21

No. **15.** High cut, kangaroo uppers, genuine elkskin soles. Will not slip on floor; extra light. The correct shoes to wear for boxing.
Pair, **$6.00**
No. **155.** High cut, elkskin soles, and will not slip on floor; soft and flexible.
Pair, **$5.00**
No. **166.** Low cut, selected leather, extra light and electric soles, men's sizes only. Pair, **$4.00**
No. **66L.** Women's. Low cut, extra light, selected leather uppers. Electric soles.
Pair, **$4.00**
No. **21.** High cut, black leather, electric soles. Sewed and turned, which makes shoes extremely light and flexible.
Pair, **$3.25**
No. **20.** Low cut. Otherwise as No. 21. Sewed and turned shoes. Pair, **$2.50**
No. **20L.** Women's. Otherwise as No. 20. Sewed and turned shoes. Pair, **$2.50**

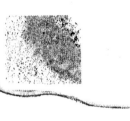

No.

STANDARD QUALITY

An article that is universally given the appellation "Standard" is thereby conceded to be the Criterion, to whic compared all other things of a similar nature. For instance, the Gold Dollar of the United States is the Standard of currency, because it must legally contain a specific proportion of pure gold, and the fact of its being Genu guaranteed by the Government Stamp thereon. As a protection to the users of this currency against counterfeitin other tricks, considerable money is expended in maintaining a Secret Service Bureau of Experts. Under the law, c manufacturers must depend to a great extent upon Trade-Marks and similar devices to protect themselves against terfeit products—without the aid of "Government Detectives" or "Public Opinion" to assist them.

Consequently the "Consumers Protection" against misrepresentation and "inferior quality" rests entirely upo integrity and responsibility of the "Manufacturer."

A. G. Spalding & Bros. have, by their rigorous attention to "Quality," for forty years, caused their Trade-Ma become known throughout the world as a Guarantee of Quality as dependable in their field as the U. S. Currency is in its

The necessity of upholding the guarantee of the Spalding Trade-Mark and maintaining the Standard Quality of Athletic Goods, is, therefore, as obvious as is the necessity of the Government in maintaining a Standard Currency.

Thus each consumer is not only insuring himself but also protecting other consumers when he assists a Re Manufacturer in upholding his Trade-Mark and all that it stands for. Therefore, we urge all users of our At Goods to assist us in maintaining the Spalding Standard of Excellence, by insisting that our Trade-Mark be p stamped on all athletic goods which they buy, because without this precaution our best efforts towards maint Standard Quality and preventing fraudulent substitution will be ineffectual.

Manufacturers of Standard Articles invariably suffer the reputation of being high-priced, and this sentiment is fo and emphasized by makers of "inferior goods," with whom low prices are the main consideration.

A manufacturer of recognized Standard Goods, with a reputation to uphold and a guarantee to protect, must earily have higher prices than a manufacturer of cheap goods, whose idea o and basis of a claim for Standard Q depends principally upon the eloquence of the salesman.

We know from experience that there is no quicksand more unstable than poverty in quality—and we avoid this quicksand by Standard Quality.

STANDARD POLICY

A Standard Quality must be inseparably linked to a Standard Policy.

Without a definite and Standard Mercantile Policy, it is impossible for a Manufacturer to long maintain a Standard Qu To market his goods through the jobber, a manufacturer must provide a profit for the jobber as well as for the dealer. To meet these conditions of Dual Profits, the manufacturer is obliged to set a proportionately high list pri his goods to the consumer.

To enable the glib salesman, when booking his orders, to figure out attractive profits to both the jobber and r these high list prices are absolutely essential; but their real purpose will have been served when the manufacture secured his order from the jobber, and the jobber has secured his order from the retailer.

However, these deceptive high list prices are not fair to the consumer, who does not, and, in reality, is not expected to pay these fancy list prices.

When the season opens for the sale of such goods, with their misleading but alluring high list prices, the r begins to realize his responsibilities, and grapples with the situation as best he can, by offering "special discounts," vary with local trade conditions.

Under this system of merchandising, the profits to both the manufacturer and the jobber are assured; but as th no stability maintained in the prices to the consumer, the keen competition amongst the local dealers invariably lea demoralized cutting of prices by which the profits of the retailer are practically eliminated.

This demoralization always reacts on the manufacturer. The jobber insists on lower, and still lower, prices. manufacturer, in his turn, meets this demand for the lowering of prices by the only way open to him, viz.: the cheap and degrading of the quality of his product.

The foregoing conditions became so intolerable that, 17 years ago, in 1899, A. G. Spalding & Bros. determined to this demoralization in the Athletic Goods Trade, and inaugurated what has since become known as "The Spalding P

The "Spalding Policy" eliminates the jobber entirely, so far as Spalding Goods are concerned, and the retail secures the supply of Spalding Athletic Goods direct from the manufacturer by which the retail dealer is assured legitimate and certain profit on all Spalding Athletic Goods, and the consumer is assured a Standard Quality rotected from imposition.

The "Spalding Policy" is decidedly for the interest and protection of the users of Athletic Goods, and acts in two

FIRST.—The user is assured of genuine Official Standard Athletic Goods.

SECOND.—As manufacturers, we can proceed with confidence in purchasing at the proper time, the very best ra materials required in the manufacture of our various goods, well ahead of their respective seasons, and this enables us to pr vide the necessary quantity and absolutely maintain the Spalding Standard of Quality.

All retail dealers handling Spalding Athletic Goods are requested to supply consumers at our regular printed ca prices—neither more nor less—the same prices that similar goods are sold for in our New York, Chicago and other

All Spalding dealers, as well as users of Spalding Athletic Goods, are treated exactly alike, and no special reb discriminations are allowed to anyone.

This, briefly, is the "Spalding Policy," which has already been in successful operation for the past 17 years, be indefinitely continued.

In other words, "The Spalding Policy" is a "square deal" for everybody.

A. G. SPALDING & BROS.

CPSIA information can be obtained at www.ICGtesting.com
Printed in the USA
BVOW05s1005030516

446561BV00024B/353/P